The Future of America: Some Topics to Consider

Bob Navarro

**2020**

**Dedicated to my Angel, Espy**

# Contents

| | |
|---|---|
| The Perspective | 7 |
| Spending for Technical Innovations | 8 |
|     Space Exploration | 9 |
|     Nuclear Research | 10 |
|     Computing Technology | 12 |
|     High-Speed Internet | 14 |
|     High-Speed Rail Transit | 16 |
|     Viable Energy Production | 17 |
|     Electronics | 18 |
|     Robotics | 19 |
|     Artificial Intelligence | 20 |
|     Information and Communications Technology | 21 |
|     Biology | 22 |
|     Chemistry | 23 |
|     Physics | 25 |
|     Mathematics | 26 |
|     Geology | 27 |
|     Weather Forecasting | 28 |
|     Medicine | 29 |
|     Mining | 31 |
|     Fire Fighting | 32 |
|     Oceanography | 33 |
| Political Issues | 34 |
|     Voting Methodology | 35 |
|     Health Care | 36 |
|     Legalization of Marijuana | 39 |
|     Women's Rights | 41 |
|     Education | 43 |
|     Defense | 44 |
|     Intelligence Gathering | 46 |
| Economic Factors | 47 |
|     Financial Systems | 48 |
|     Home Building | 50 |
|     Transportation | 52 |
|     Infrastructure | 53 |
|     Agriculture | 54 |
|     Drivers for Economics | 55 |
|     Taxation | 56 |
|     Trade | 57 |
|     Globalization | 58 |
|     Unemployment | 59 |
|     Automation | 60 |
| Social Issues | 62 |
|     Substance Abuse | 63 |

|  |  |
|---|---|
| Psychology and Psychiatry | 64 |
| Prison Reform | 67 |
| The Homeless Problem | 68 |
| Proliferation of Firearms | 69 |
| Police Forces | 71 |
| Malnutrition | 74 |
| Poverty | 76 |
| Population Ageing | 77 |
| Immigration | 78 |
| Racism | 79 |
| Crime | 83 |
| Environmental Concerns | 84 |
| Dealing with the Environment | 85 |
| Destruction of the Oceans | 86 |
| Global Warming | 90 |
| Pollution | 92 |
| Atmospheric Changes | 94 |
| Damaging Chemical Effects | 95 |
| Biological Threats | 96 |
| Nuclear Waste Accumulation | 98 |
| The Myth of Clean Coal | 99 |
| The Problem with Oil | 101 |
| Natural Gas is Not the Answer | 104 |
| No More Nuclear Fission Plants | 105 |
| Genetic Engineering | 107 |
| Overconsumption | 108 |
| Global Problems | 110 |
| Terrorism | 111 |
| Nuclear Proliferation | 115 |
| Increasing Population | 117 |
| Food Shortages | 119 |
| Lack of Fresh Water | 121 |
| Unequal Distribution of Wealth | 124 |
| Sex Exploitation and Slavery | 125 |
| Decimation of Forests | 126 |
| Desertification | 129 |
| Warfare | 131 |
| Drug Trafficking | 134 |
| Weapon Development | 138 |
| Biological Weapons | 139 |
| Chemical Weapons | 142 |
| Radiological Weapons | 143 |
| Nuclear Weapons | 144 |
| Apocalyptic Scenarios | 146 |
| Decreasing Biodiversity | 147 |
| Bees, Bats and Amphibians | 148 |

| | |
|---|---:|
| Worldwide Pandemic | 149 |
| Nuclear Holocaust | 151 |
| Runaway Greenhouse | 155 |
| The Future of America | 157 |
| Bibliography | 158 |

# The Perspective

As America ventures into the third decade of the 21st century, investing in the United States economy will make the country stronger, reduce unemployment by creating jobs, will revitalize key industries, and even create new manufacturing companies. There is a great potential for the United States to launch new projects by investing in the infrastructure and the environment, and in new technologies that will produce new industries and create jobs for the population. The critical point in the nation has been reached where it is very important to do things that help our population survive and thrive. In doing so we will also help the rest of the world, especially if they model us in pursuing the same goals.

The Challenges

Several forces are operating on humanity, which if left unattended could result in dire consequences for all living entities on the planet. These are acting as time bombs with fuses that are already lighted and ready to explode in our midst unless corrective actions are undertaken by all of us to either stop them or to prevent them from happening. All of these forces require collective agreements, cooperation and participation, for without the understanding that is required on a global basis, all fragmented decisions and deeds undertaken by only a few will not solve the major problems—nor deter the destructive impacts, which will surely occur as a result of inaction. Many forces are in play, any of which can be the cause of a great calamity in the well-being of the earth. Some of these forces are already making themselves felt. Although the problems and solutions that are presented in this book do not represent an exhaustive list, they do point to some of the imminent dangers as well as opportunities for all human beings on this planet.

The manifestation of these dangers to our civilization is rooted in the inherent inward malfunctioning of our brains. All of the attendant psychological fragmentations, socially invented differences and unchecked emotional disorders are creating the conditions in which all of these ills can multiply rapidly without any recourse or remedying—much less rectifying—the causes of detrimental outcomes. These problems are interrelated and they impact one another. But, it is in the synergy effects of all these time bombs and the resulting phenomena that pose the greatest danger to human survival. We waste human capital and potential in keeping the status quo. Spending trillions of dollars on war instead of investing in the infrastructure and the environment will lead to a marked decline in cities, roadways and buildings. Lack of cures means that endemics and pandemics will result that potentially will affect everyone. The critical point in the world has been reached for the survival of the population. We must act now.

**Spending for Technical Innovations**

# Space Exploration

## Overview

Given the return on investment of the previous space program for the moon project, a renewal of a greatly enhanced space program, especially for the Mars mission, will lead to even more innovations that will in turn produce benefits for the entire economy. Seven different categories of space exploration can be pursued, as well as an increase in funding for the International Space Station (ISS). These are more unmanned missions to the moon, Mars, other planets, asteroids, comets, moons of other planets and the sun. New rocket technology also needs to be developed to provide more powerful engines that can carry heavy payloads as well as astronauts. Financially, the Mars project can be accomplished by spending as little as 2½% of what is spent on defense.

## History

In the previous space program, several technological applications emerged from the research and technological breakthroughs that occurred. The flight computer design started the research into integrated circuits. The fuel cell development led to a new source of producing electrical energy. Computer-controlled machining used in fabricating structural components led to computer-aided manufacturing processes. Many of our technological advances are due largely to the Apollo Moon Project. Over 1,650 spin-off products were produced from the NASA innovations during the moon project, including advances in computer technology, the environment, agriculture enhancements, medical techniques, transportation and recreational activities. Other significant spin-offs that emerged from the moon space program were video enhancing and analysis systems, water purification systems, solar energy devices, and structural analysis software. It was a return on investment that was well worth doing. Just think of the innovations that could come out of the Mars project.

## The Case for Space Exploration

Several advances in space exploration need to be investigated further, especially alternative sources of propulsion and energy sources. The types of these developments include starships with sails that are powered by light, laser communication systems, atomic navigation systems, advanced robotic systems for exploring, more research on weightlessness effects on the human body, advances in slowing down metabolism for long space journeys, developing protection against harmful radiation, faster and more powerful rockets, extending the list of crops that can be grown in space, and the development of enhanced recovery systems to provide air and water for astronauts.

# Nuclear Research

## Super Collider

A superconducting super collider (SSC) project was started in Waxahachie, Texas in the mid 1980s. The particle accelerator was set to be the world's largest and most energetic collider, with a circumference of 54 miles and an energy of 20 teravolts per proton. The project cost was stated to be $4.4 billion. President Ronald Reagan supported the project as did his successor, President George H. W. Bush. But, Congress cancelled the project in 1993 after $2 billion had been spent, and after 14 miles of tunnels and 17 shafts to the surface had been dug—with 20% of the construction done and 45% of the circumference dug. In spite of the fact that the SSC would have had 5 times the power of the LHC in Europe, the absolutely mistaken belief was that many smaller scientific experiments of equal merit could be funded for the same cost. President Bill Clinton tried to prevent the cancellation by asking Congress to continue to support the SSC project because abandoning it would signal that the United States was compromising its position of leadership in basic science. The budget cancellation was viewed as a disregard for basic funding—not just only for science research—but for the general provision of adequate education, healthcare, transportation and communication infrastructure, and criminal justice and law enforcement.

If all had gone according to plan, the SSC project would have found the Higgs particle earlier than the LHC in Europe, as well as research into super symmetry and dark matter. But, a lack of will killed the project. However, reviving the SSC project in the same location by building a linear accelerator could provide energies of up to 300 teravolts—something that would potentially yield more secrets of the fundamental structure of matter. The economic benefits would generate more than 13,000 jobs, which in turn would greatly benefit the local communities. The new knowledge that can be gained from this renewed SSC project could be used for peaceful means for humankind.

## Fusion Power

The United States, the European Union, China, India, Russia, Japan and South Korea signed an accord in 2006 to build a $12.8 billion experimental fusion reactor at Cadarache, France aimed at revolutionizing global energy use for future generations. The project, called International Thermonuclear Experimental Reactor (ITER), is currently being funded by the European Commission, which has provided 1.4 billion euros for the international commitment because the European governments are unwilling to fund it at present. The ITER project seeks to replicate the processes at the core of stars and the sun to provide a potential source of cheap, abundant and carbon-free fuel. Construction of ITER began in 2012. Another ongoing project to create nuclear fusion is the National Ignition Facility (NIF) located at the California Livermore National Laboratory. Still another nuclear fusion project is the Shiva Star Facility located at Kirtland Air Force base in New Mexico.

Funding for fusion research could mean a tremendous return if a sustainable method of generating fusion nuclear power for an energy source is discovered. It would also aid the environment since a fusion nuclear process will not generate the harmful and toxic radioactive waste materials that nuclear fission produces. Also, there is no possibility of a catastrophic accident in a fusion reactor resulting in major release of radioactivity to the environment or injury to people—unlike fission reactors.

Fusion power would provide more energy than any fuel-consuming energy source currently in use. The source of its fuel is deuterium, an element that exists abundantly in the Earth's ocean. Fusion reactors could potentially supply the world's energy needs for millions of years. Another aspect of fusion energy is that the cost of production does not suffer from diseconomies of scale. With fusion energy the production cost will not increase much even if large numbers of plants are built, because the raw resource, which is seawater, is abundant.

Fusion power could also be applied to problems such as those of fresh water shortages. In desalination plants, seawater can be purified through distillation or reverse osmosis—but these processes are energy intensive. Fusion power to run desalination plants would alleviate the severe effects of drought, especially in areas such as California and the Southwest. Fusion power could also be used in interstellar space where solar energy is not available.

Current fusion research projects in the United States are being conducted at the Lawrence Livermore National Laboratory in California. However, more funding needs to be applied to accelerate the research that is needed to create the breakthroughs in fusion technology. This is a very critical issue, especially since the earth is becoming warmer as the $CO_2$ levels rise as a result of gas, oil and coal-powered emissions. Energy created from fusion power sources can provide a virtually inexhaustible, safe, environmentally friendly and universally available supply to meet humanity's energy needs for a very long time.

Finally, the greatest benefit of pursuing nuclear fusion is that it will greatly alleviate the climate crisis that we now face by global warming. It will reduce the reliance on coal, gas and oil facilities that currently exist to provide power. Coal is the worst substance to be burning, with oil being a second worst. As we edge closer to the 2-degree increase in global temperature, we already see the evidence of climate changes such as the melting of the Arctic and Antarctic ice caps, the disappearance of major glaciers, fiercer storms, hotter summer temperatures, droughts and flooding. Without any major advances in alternative fuels, we will only make matters worse through the continued burning of dangerous fuels.

# Computing Technology

Funding for advancement in supercomputing technology will aid the fields of weather forecasting, quantum mechanics, molecular modeling and physical simulations—such as studies of the early moments of the beginning of the universe. Supercomputers can also assist in determining airplane and spacecraft aerodynamics, code breaking, human cerebral cortex modeling and probabilistic analysis. In terms of the World Wide Web, there are five areas that can be researched: databases, security, clouds, network enhancement and advanced web development. In addition, parallel computing should be further advanced to provide the high-speed capabilities needed for weather prediction, stock market analyses, medical research and war-gaming exercises.

Supercomputers can be further enhanced to provide even faster computations that will assist in weather forecasting, biological and DNA modeling, biometric innovations, nuclear theoretical analysis, data mining, software engineering and other large-scale projects that require fast processing speeds. Databases can be developed so that they encompass much more data and search capabilities—and so that they can be linked together to provide data analysis on a wider scale. Cyber security enhancements can be developed to prevent hacking and the spread of malware such as worms, viruses and bugs. Grid computing can also be tightened up to secure member nodes from malicious attacks.

Cloud computing can be made much more granular to handle time-dependent workloads. Cloud resources can be further geographically distributed to numerous locations to provide thousands or even millions of connections. Network enhancements can be developed so that a huge numbers of computers can be connected to solve very complex problems. Network enhancement—in conjunction with excellent security—can eliminate the antiquated methods of voting that exist in the country. Electronic governance can be improved significantly to deliver government services and exchange of information as well as communication transactions to both individual customers as well as businesses.

Advanced web development can be done to create better search engines as more and more information becomes available on the Internet. The present web search engines are barely adequate for extensive searches, and increases in speed will be needed to thoroughly search the content that is available. A greater collaboration among Internet users, content providers and enterprises will be required to handle the massive amounts of data. The creation of semantic webs will have the ability to select the pages that a user really wants or needs to see through the use of metadata. Further development of the web will create capabilities of knowledge management to provide almost instant access to just about any inquiry on any subject matter that exists.

Parallel computing can be increased so that pervasive computing can be carried out simultaneously—and fast. Parallelism currently has physical constraints that prevent scaling. Faster multi-core processors need to be built with less power consumption and heat generation to create clusters for multiple processing. Better methods of communication and synchronization need to be developed to provide a better integration of subtasks. The advancement and development of new computer languages will also be required. These high performance innovations with parallel computing can be used by multimedia, computer vision, communications, automobiles, image processing, medical research, photography, robotics, gaming models, speech recognition and translation, aerial vehicles, wireless communication, soft computing and aspect-oriented programming. The potential is unlimited, and its development will create many new applications—as well as jobs.

Further miniaturization of computers can be further advanced through new processors. This will create a whole new world of cellular phones, tablets and watches. In particular, quantum and nano computing advances will make possible whole new areas in information technology, especially with respect to electronic learning. It can even be applied to ontology as robotics in combination with computer systems to create synergetic entities that more closely model human behavior.

The most promising computer innovation is with respect to quantum based computing. These offer possibilities of speeds that dwarf current computing capabilities. Funding for research into these types of computers will enable better computational models for weather forecasting, business projections, stock market analyses and faster space exploration data transmissions for space vehicles relaying data back to earth.

# High-Speed Internet

Overview

5G networks are digital cellular networks in which the service area covered by providers is divided into small geographical areas called cells. Analog signals are digitized in the telephone, and are converted to digital signals and then are transmitted as a stream of bits. All the 5G wireless devices in a cell communicate by radio waves with a local antenna array and automated transceiver in the cell. The local antennas are connected with the telephone network and the Internet by a high bandwidth optical fiber or wireless connection. A mobile device crossing from one cell to another is automatically handed off to the new cell.

Verizon and a few others are using millimeter waves, which have shorter range than microwaves. Therefore, the cells are limited to a smaller size. Millimeter waves have difficulty traversing many walls and windows, so indoor coverage is limited. Millimeter wave antennas are also smaller than the large antennas that are used in previous cellular networks.

The Technology

5G is the fifth generation wireless technology for digital cellular networks that has begun wide deployment. Like previous standards the covered areas are divided into regions called cells, serviced by individual antennas. Virtually every major telecommunication service provider is deploying antennas or intends to deploy them. The frequency spectrum of 5G is divided into millimeter waves, which are mid-band and low-band. The reach is short, so more cells are required. 5G mid-band is the most widely deployed, and exists in over 20 networks. Many areas can be covered simply by upgrading existing towers, which lowers the cost.

5G low-band offers an increased capacity for the Internet. Although the performance will improve, it cannot be much higher because of latency. The latency in equipment (between a phone and a tower) is on the average latency about 30 milliseconds. Adding servers close to the towers can bring latency down to between 10 to 20 milliseconds. Currently, a lower latency of 1 millisecond, is years away and does not include the time needed to reach the server.

The Implementation

The wireless industry wants to build some 800,000 5G small cells by 2026. Although apprenticeship efforts, in-house training and academic and technical training partnerships are underway, they won't be enough to meet the demand for skilled technicians. This lack of a properly skilled workforce is a huge obstacle for implementing 5G. This is a definite requirement in order to build the super-fast 5G networks that will span the country, powering everything from smart cities to remote surgeries. At present, the United States needs to train an additional 20,000 tower climbers to install the 5G equipment—a doubling of the current workforce.

The 5G next-generation wireless networks, made up of thousands of tightly clustered suitcase-sized cell sites, are already coming online in a several cities, such as Minneapolis, Minnesota and Sacramento, California. They are 100 times faster than current networks and will radically reshape the global economy, ushering in a new era of connected devices, driverless cars and enhanced telemedicine.

However, the United States is not only facing a shortage of tower climbers, but many other workers who are skilled enough to roll out the infrastructure of wireless companies. To implement the economic promise of this new Internet technology, a broader network-building process is required, which includes laying fiber, climbing cell towers and placing hundreds of thousands of smaller pieces of infrastructure known as small cells, something that will require 100,000 new jobs to accomplish the task. Significant investments are needed in building up a more robust digital infrastructure of fiber optic networks that are important to facilitate the large-scale deployment of 5G, with costs amounting to hundreds of billions of dollars.

The federal government must provide some sort of broader, more uniform federal support for workforce reskilling. Without this funding, it will be very hard to fully deploy next-generation wireless technology nationwide, and to exert influence over the broader global 5G industry. But, it requires a massive apprenticeship effort with more resources to alleviate the worker shortfall.

## High-Speed Rail Transit

The construction of high-speed rail transit systems will provide a big boost in transportation of people and goods. At least three coast-to-coast high-speed railways should be built to connect the West coast with the East coast of the United States. At least three North-to-South high-speed railways are also needed to provide better transport service from the important centers of the North such as Seattle and Portland to Southern cities such as Los Angeles and San Diego. Similarly, high-speed railways that link New York and Washington, D.C. to Miami and Atlanta will create many possibilities. Intercity high-speed railway connections are also important, such as commuter trains between New York City and Washington, D.C. Speeds of 150 mph or more will lessen travel times considerably for both passenger travel and freight services. The speed can be increased considerably, with speeds up to 300 mph or more being possible, with adequate safeguards to prevent accidents along the rail lines.

The construction of these railway systems will require additional building projects such as overpasses, tunnels and bridges, especially through urban areas. All of these will create many jobs, with the benefit being that of a closer connected transportation grid across the entire country. New tracks that are required for high-speed trains must also be built. High-speed rail transport operates significantly faster than traditional rail traffic, using an integrated system of specialized rolling stock and dedicated tracks. Most of the world is investing in high-speed trains, and it is only in the United States that there is an insufficient lack of funds to develop this type of transportation system.

In 1992, Congress passed the Amtrak Authorization and Development Act to focus on Amtrak's service improvement on the segment between Boston and New York City. The primary objectives were to electrify the line north of New Haven, Connecticut, and to replace the Metroliners with new trains to achieve shorter travel time. The new service linked Boston, New York City, Philadelphia, Baltimore, and Washington DC. However, the United States currently has only one high speed rail line under construction in California, and a planned one in Texas. High-speed rail projects are also underway in the Pacific Northwest, Midwest and Southeast, as well as upgrades on the high-speed Northeast Corridor and in Florida. But, federal funding is lacking, and a planned high-speed rail line between Los Angeles and San Francisco was cancelled.

With high speed rail there is an increase in accessibility within cities. It allows for urban regeneration, accessibility in cities, and efficient inter-city relationships. Better inter-city relationships lead to high level services to companies, advanced technology, and marketing. The most important effect of high speed rail is the increase of accessibility due to shorter travel times. High speed rail lines can create long distance routes which in many cases cater to business travelers. However, there have also been short distance routes that have revolutionized the concepts of high speed rail. Using both longer distance and shorter distance rail allows for the best case of economic development, widening the labor and residential market of a metropolitan area and extending it to smaller cities. But government funding is necessary to offset the high initial costs.

# Viable Energy Production

Solar power, wind power, geothermal power, hybrid and electric cars, and aggressive energy efficiency are climate solutions that are safer, cheaper, faster, more secure, and less wasteful than nuclear power, gas, oil and coal. The United States needs a massive influx of investment in these solutions if we are to avoid the worst consequences of climate change. The investment in alternative energy sources is also necessary to enjoy energy security, jump-start our economy, create jobs, and work to lead the world in development of clean energy. The United States should lead by example and encourage poor countries to invest in safe energy technology. Energy production promises to be a goldmine for the United States. The various forms of energy production that are environmentally safe that can be exploited are solar power, wind power, ocean wave power, thermal facilities and battery power, such as for automobiles and homes.

The most important type is that of renewable energy. But, government funding has been cut back and investors have been reluctant to back these types of energy production because of their initial cost. Nevertheless, solar farms and wind turbine generators are sustainable energy sources in contrast to coal, oil and gas energy generation, which only add to the already high levels of $CO_2$ in the atmosphere. Battery power can also be used for homes, businesses and automobiles. Water wave and tidal systems offer renewable sources of energy. Lasers that ionize gases to convert them into energy are also useful ventures that can be pursued. But, fusion power generation is the ultimate source because it is unlimited and clean.

Helium, is another great source of energy—although it is currently only available in sufficient quantities on the moon. But, with advances in transport technology, it may be possible to deliver abundant quantities to earth via some type of shuttle system. Fuel cells that were developed during the quest to the moon are an energy source that can be used almost anywhere. Biofuels offer another interesting source for energy production. Still another avenue of energy production is that of harnessing the earth's heat. All of these possibilities of energy production can be done with enough funding and perseverance. All that is lacking is the will to do it. With the climate crisis, which is at hand, developing more coal, gas, oil facilities and nuclear fission plants will only add to the global warming and toxic waste problems that already exist.

# Electronics

The best electronic technologies to pursue are nanotechnology, miniaturization and quantum electronics. Multiple molecular patterns that can be fitted within a single material enable new nanoscale architectures to be built. Miniature electro-optical switches can bridge the gap between light and electricity. Infrared and optical masers that can be built by using quantum electronics can extend the range of frequencies for amplifiers and oscillators, which would allow spectroscopy at much higher resolutions.

Superconducting films that are laid on top of silicon offer another type of electronics breakthrough because these superconductors conduct electricity without resistance, and because silicon is abundantly available and inexpensive. Liquid metals are also promising to create flexible and reconfigurable soft circuit systems, such as 3D electronic displays and components. Photonics-based circuits offer another great potential by using a coupling of light with electrons.

Lithium ion batteries have a great potential, especially if they can be charged and discharged many times before they reach their end of life. Such batteries are ideal for handheld electronic devices as well as for electric vehicles. Another area of research is that of artificial neurons that store and process data. These artificial neurons are energy efficient, ultra-dense neuromorphic technologies that can be used for cognitive computing.

The Mars project would probably accelerate the push to develop new electronic equipment, and would undoubtedly create breakthroughs in the electronics industry.

# Robotics

Robots will have a significant presence at work and at home. Factories with advanced manufacturing robots will increase productivity to new levels, especially with 7 by 24 operations. However, newer projects will require more advanced and cost-efficient robots to run the factories of the future. Current robots are very effective for precise and repetitive work, but are used only in carefully designed settings. They cannot easily adapt to a new task, and cannot cope with an unfamiliar or uncertain situation.

New techniques and algorithms must be developed to enable robots to learn much more quickly and effectively. Deep learning, which uses large simulated neural networks, will prove to be indispensable for training robots to understand the contents of images, video, and audio—as well as how to see, grasp, and reason. Other techniques that have to be developed are robots that share the knowledge that they have acquired with other robots. This will require the acceleration of the learning process, instantly allowing a robot to benefit from the efforts of other robots. This learning process can be extended so that even two completely different robots can teach each other how to recognize a particular object or perform a new task.

Drone technology can be used to help automate air traffic control for automated vehicles. Smart and autonomous drones can be used in many industries, especially ones where automated surveillance and inspection are necessary. More sophisticated military drones are also possible to detect and eliminate terrorist camps and installations.

In terms of personal robots, more capable and cheaper hardware and software will provide an engaging personal touch. Robotic companions and helpers at present have only limited roles, such as meeting and greeting people at stores. Fully functional robot cars on our highways won't crash into each other, and won't need the bumper bars or steel cages, so they will be more comfortable and lighter. Most cars will be electric, and will not need parking spots because they will drop us where we want to go to and pick us up when we are ready. We won't even need to own our own cars, because transportation will be available on demand. We also won't need speed limits, so distance will be less of a barrier, thus enabling us to leave the cities and suburbs.

Medicine will advance tremendously through robotics. Bionic eyes will help people with macular degeneration in people who are losing their eyesight by using AI algorithms and computer vision algorithms. Bionic ears will help people with hearing loss. Bionic hands will enable people who have lost limbs to perform complex tasks. Bionic legs will allow paraplegics to walk, run and move about normally.

All of these robot advances require research funding so that they can be integrated with AI technology to produce smart robots. The possibilities are endless and unlimited for robotics if we just invest enough money to develop their capabilities. Again, the Mars project is very suitable to develop the new robotic technologies.

## Artificial Intelligence

Artificial intelligence (AI) research into whole-brain simulations offer a very promising return on investment, especially with respect to robots. Better algorithms and smarter computers will be one benefit of increased funding for AI projects, especially in the areas of computer vision and speech recognition. AI can be used to monitor credit card systems for fraudulent behavior, high frequency stock trading and for detecting cyber security threats. It can be used to aid in transportation, to provide better medical service by diagnosing illnesses and analyzing pharmaceuticals, by managing power grids and by enhancing deep learning for robots. Deep learning uses large data sets, machine learning algorithms and deep neural networks to teach the AI how to perform a particular set of tasks. Rather than programming complex rules and strategies, data is fed so that the AI learns from its own mistakes and improves its learning over time. Possessing a more intuitive approach to problem solving allows AI to succeed in highly complex environments. Actions with high levels of unpredictability, such as talking, driving, serving as a soldier, which are unmanageable for AI, can be solved by deep learning. AI can manage complex, data intensive tasks. Deep learning AI can also be used for transportation, medical and military robots.

Deep learning represents a paradigm shift in the relationship humans have with their technological creations. It results in AI that displays unpredictable behavior. The goal is to anticipate and control for as many possible states a device could find itself in. Surprises mean that the design has deviated from its intended behavior, and thus requires a fix. AI robots will continue to learn and to improve in ways that are unknown at present. Other types of AI can be designed to benefit humanity by surpassing our abilities in highly complex tasks, such as diagnosing illness, researching pharmaceuticals, managing power grids, and protecting against cyber threats. But, all this must be done by drafting ethics standards for robotics and AI. And, this area is precisely where much money needs to be spent so that machines do not overpower their creators.

Once again, the Mars project is a perfect opportunity to develop advanced robotics that are using AI, especially in time sensitive decisions that require instant feedback, which cannot be done by earth-based commands because of time delays.

# Information and Communications Technology

Information and communications technology incorporates networks, television, smart phones, Wi-Fi, the Internet, computers and tablets. Online networking websites, such as Facebook, Twitter and LinkedIn, are becoming the most popular means of instant communication. These sites allow users to communicate with friends, family and clients instantaneously. You can add images, update your status, start a fan page for your business, write notes, and send personal messages. However, faster and cheaper techniques are needed to handle the ever-increasing amount of traffic and information.

Some of the required information and communications advances will involve the following:

- Virtualized and more open source network computing platforms and architecture
- New investments in fiber to handle high definition video, faster wireless technology, streaming, podcast and other broadband services
- Upgrades to 5G wireless broadband technology to relieve network congestion, increase energy efficiency, reduce cost, increase reliability, and to provide connection to billions of people and devices.
- Everywhere connectivity
- Cognitive networks to deal with embedded devices, mobile users, enterprises, contextual information, network protocols and location information
- Enhanced cyber security to protect devices and endpoints
- Smarter cellphones and connected sensors
- Keeping network neutrality to maintain no connection blocking, bandwidth transparency, universal connectivity, and best effort service.
- Molecular communications where bio nano machines communicate to perform coordinated actions
- Environmentally friendly batteries, renewable energy sources and intelligent management of power systems

Both industry and government must work together to create the needed information and communications environments. Funding should be provided by the government to stimulate the research and innovations in information and communications technologies. This includes investments in new towers, satellites, fiber optics and network systems.

# Biology

Biological endeavors that can provide great benefits include DNA mapping techniques and blood type research. The acquisition of new biological diversity such as through new enzymes, new molecular compounds, in vitro evolution, and alteration of microbes offer tremendous opportunities for better health management. Synthetic biology, manipulation of biological systems and DNA synthesis and genetic breeding offer a new generation of advances for prevention of diseases. The search for previously unrecognized naturally occurring biological diversity can produce new drugs as well as new sources for medical, agricultural and industrial uses. Genetic engineering of viruses can alter their harmful effects. RNA interference can produce new and more viable strains of plants and animals by preventing tumors and other maladies.

Systems biology can be used to study complex interactions involving DNA, RNA and proteins. Bio pharming can also be used to harvest bioactive molecules from mass-cultured organisms and crops for use as ingredients in industrial products and pharmaceuticals such as vaccines. Microencapsulation to envelop small solid particles, liquid droplets, or gas bubbles with a protective coating can produce miniature containers that protect their contents from evaporation, oxidation, and contamination and which can be engineered with a variety of unique release mechanisms. These can be controlled and delayed as targeted releases to better counter many diseases in a systematic manner.

Gene therapy technology uses healthy genes to treat or prevent disease by inserting a gene into a genome to replace an abnormal disease-causing gene. More progress needs to be made to advance the research so that it can become a standard care option for any individual disorder. Targeting biologically active materials to specific locations in the body will reduce the exposure of non-target tissues to drugs. Also, the convergence of bio-, nano-, and information technologies can produce a transformation that can be as powerful as the Industrial Revolution. We must continue our ability to modify fundamental biological processes and advance them so that we will be able to devise additional ways to manipulate them—including the processes of cognition, development, reproduction and inheritance.

# Chemistry

Great advances in chemistry can be made through the creation of new plastics and hybrid materials. Combinatorial chemistry can create large numbers of synthetic compounds to create new drugs. Aerosol technology can be improved to protect forests from damage and defoliation caused by insects. Liquid metals can also propel future electronics products. $CO_2$ gases can be carbon-captured before they are released to the atmosphere and can be converted to produce electricity. Photo organic chemistry on water surfaces can be used to form new organic molecules. Radiation chemistry that uses gamma radiation, lasers and X-rays can result in new chemical components such as radioisotopes, hydrocarbons, new crystal structures and other exotic materials. Research into inorganic chemistry also offers many intriguing possibilities for use in agriculture, fuels and medications.

Innovation is the backbone of the American economy and well-being. Since WWII, nearly half of the GDP growth has resulted from investments in research and development (R&D). Federal support of R&D opens new areas of technology, and provides a path to long-term economic growth because of high-impact, fundamental discoveries that spawn entire industries. Federal support of R&D increases national security and provides knowledge to inform local, state and national decisions by providing the means to weigh options and to evaluate their effectiveness.

Federally-funded universities and government laboratories generally work on new technologies in the earliest stages while industry brings more mature advances to the marketplace. Curiosity-driven and high-risk, high impact research has produced discoveries that have spawned entire new industries. Such long-term work needs to be supported by government funding because the time frames needed to complete the work extends beyond those reasonable for industry to consider.

Given the long-term nature of research, predictable and sustained federal funding is critical to our technology driven economy, but federal research support as a percentage of GDP has shrunk, negatively impacting many areas of science and technology, especially with regard to research in chemistry. The impact of these cuts has been exacerbated by uncertainty in the federal budget decision process. Unpredictable budgets lead to a high turnover of trained scientists and a loss of the operational infrastructure critical for success.

Policymakers need to invest in long-term economic growth by setting funding levels that support R&D. To ensure the scientific foundation is laid for the economy of the future, the United States must reverse the path that has taken us to our current low of federal R&D investment. The best way to achieve American preeminence is to bolster R&D investments. Government support of curiosity-driven research is essential in the process of providing American industry with the science to develop products to enable economic growth.

Successful, later-stage technology transfer and development programs are also necessary. Funding of shared facilities, methods development, equipment, indirect costs associated with the conduct of funded research, and other resources is essential for scientific competitiveness. This is because the government plays an essential role in targeting R&D dollars to areas of critical need, including national security, energy production, food growth, and public health. Research funding also enables the specialized training of scientists and engineers that will be necessary for next generation advances and it is required to train future generations. Chemistry is the basis of almost every new endeavor that affects humans, and it must be funded adequately.

# Physics

Breakthroughs in physics involve advances in electro-optics technology and enhanced cosmology research. But, government funds are needed for all kinds of physics research that advances our understanding of the world we live in, that includes and educates an increasingly diverse group of scientists, and that benefits everyone in society. It can bring about technological advances that permeate everyday life in ways that increase living for everyone. However, the biggest component of research and development funding in the United States is the military, and increasingly vast sums are being spent on classified research. In contrast, theoretical physics has very little funding. Money for cosmology research is limited, and even money for space research and exploration is relatively small.

In the past huge funds were allocated for the Manhattan Project that developed the atom bomb, and for the Radiation Laboratory at MIT that developed radar systems and microwave electronic devices. In more recent times, substantial funds were made available to accomplish the man-on-the-moon project, the International Space Station and the Space Shuttle program. But, since that era, funds have been continually cut to the point where the United States no longer has any capability to place people in space. Cuts geared towards placing astronauts on the moon again have completely shut those projects down. Even funding for the manned exploration of Mars has slowed to a trickle, with the earliest venture planned not earlier than 2035. Our scientists can accomplish a lot more if they are given adequate financial support. Instead, downsizing has occurred, and much unemployment has been created for these gifted and trained scientists who possess advanced degrees. They have been relegated to being professors at universities, which have limited funding for the type of research that is needed to obtain breakthroughs in physics. These individuals are not using their scientific talent, knowledge and experience to their fullest extent.

Military funding has produced technological advances that have produced superior weapons such as the stealth aircraft, precision-guided bombs and drones. In some cases, military research funding has led to societal advances, such as the development of the Internet, integrated circuits, microprocessors, computers, satellites, GPS and smart appliances. But, a better motivation is to increase research funding for its own sake—for the greater good. More government grants are needed for universities, corporations, non-profit organizations and individual scientists to promote basic research in physics because it is important to explore the unknown—and because basic scientific research benefits all of society. While it is not possible to predict the results of research projects or the long-term impacts of those results on society, they should be undertaken because of the potential for significant discoveries that can benefit everyone—not just the military.

## Mathematics

Mathematics deserves public funding because many of the great scientific advances have been built on mathematical discoveries. For example, the discovery of the square root of negative numbers, underlies a huge section of modern technology—from the design of circuits, airplanes and skyscrapers, to the construction of economic and financial models, and to robotics. Another example is quantum mechanics, which is responsible for much of the electronics that exists today, and the development of calculus that has been used everywhere. Still another example is the mathematical theory behind electromagnetics, Fourier analysis and circuit theory, which are responsible for the comfortable style of living that everyone enjoys today—especially that of electricity. Computer science would not exist today if it were not for advances that were made in mathematics, such as algorithms and programming theory. Pure mathematics research is very important, especially in fields such as group theory, knot theory and number theory. However, at present funding is applied mostly to mathematicians who are going to teach mathematics to other mathematicians. It is important to note that mathematics has been incredibly effective in describing the world. While research into pure mathematics may not yield immediate payoffs, there is always the possibility of a fundamental discovery in mathematics that could produce immeasurable results.

# Geology

Because geology deals with the earth's physical structure, its history and the processes that act on it, it is an important subject in terms of understanding major events such as earthquakes, volcanic eruptions, landslides and floods. Since these events represent hazardous conditions for people, it is wise to study the structures in greater detail to at least forecast warnings of imminent dangers. Better maps of areas that have been flooded before can predict where these may be flooded again to provide better flood protection and prevention.

Geological studies are very important in determining effects from oil that has been pumped from wells, natural gas that has been removed from the earth, metals that have been dug out from mines, and water that has been drawn from streams and underground water systems. Climate change studies are important to obtain knowledge of how past climate changes have affected the earth, especially with regard to glaciers, lava flows, droughts and floods. Money has to be allocated to natural resource companies, environmental companies, non-profit organizations and universities, as well as for grants for the subjects of paleontology, mineralogy, hydrology and volcanology.

# Weather Forecasting

Weather forecasting needs to be improved to prevent many of the tragedies that now occur because of a lack of warning systems. Enhanced satellites, tornado sensors, hurricane tracking systems, and storm tracking techniques can be developed to provide plenty of time to warn people in the affected areas, thus saving lives. Stronger and more frequent weather extremes will likely occur under climate change so improved weather prediction will be vital to giving communities more time to prepare for dangerous storms. New Doppler radar technology that will allow forecasters to better track extreme weather, improvements to satellite technology that provides a better view of the atmosphere, and computer models that run on more powerful supercomputers are all areas that need to be improved.

Phased array radars need to be installed all around the country to replace outdated parabolic dishes that must be mechanically turned. A phased-array radar sends out multiple beams simultaneously, eliminating the need to tilt antennas, thus decreasing the time between scans of storms. This improvement will allow the viewing of rapidly evolving changes in thunderstorm circulations, and to more quickly detect the changes that cause tornadoes. Phased-array radar can gather storm information not currently available, such as fast changes in wind fields, which can precede rapid changes in storm intensity. Phased-array technology could extend tornado warnings by having four panels emitting and receiving radio waves to provide a 360-degree view of the atmosphere—one each for the North, South, East and West. But, at present funding levels, it will be years before phased array radars are installed across the country.

Satellites are very important to provide broader data that supplement the information that is obtained from radar. Weather satellites supply the majority of the data for daily and long-range forecasts, and they are critical in providing alerts of severe weather potential multiple days in advance. To improve the delivery of this essential intelligence, deployment of new technologies must be done, especially because of climate change. Without more detailed satellite observations, extending the range of accurate weather forecasts, especially for hurricanes, will be severely restricted. More geostationary satellites to transmit continuous views of the earth's surface, and polar satellites, which provide more detailed observations of the temperature and humidity of different layers of the atmosphere are urgently needed. In conjunction with these satellites, advanced microwave and infrared sensors are required to provide improved three-dimensional information on the atmosphere's lightning, temperature, pressure and moisture—predictors of very strong storms such as category 4 and 5 tornadoes. Faster supercomputers are definitely necessary to process more grid data for forecasting models. With greater funding for weather forecasting it will be possible to extend severe weather warnings beyond the current limits so that populations can seek shelter to avoid loss of lives.

# Medicine

Great strides can be made in the field of medicine with expanded research into diseases such as cancer, alzheimers, AIDS, Sika virus and Ebola. Drugs can be made more powerful with less side effects so that they can assist in the treatment of various ailments. Hospital enhancements can be achieved to adequately staff them with well-trained doctors and nurses. Biotechnology can be markedly improved to tackle damages to immune systems, to develop new scanning techniques, to map out the genes and isolate those that cause hereditary diseases, and to increase life-saving techniques—both in the field and at hospitals.

More funding should be made available for the complete sequencing of the human genome for a better understanding of the complex bacterial systems that live in and on our bodies. Stem cell research needs to be expanded because these can be programmed to become any type of cell in the body. Stem cells have an enormous potential for curing diseases and for repairing damaged tissues, especially for heart ailments and eye diseases. More effective drugs need to be developed to combat the spread of HIV, and more effective drugs that work at the molecular level will be required to conquer cancer in its many forms.

Minimal invasive surgeries of all types need to be developed to produce less pain, smaller scars and faster recovery times. Better anesthetics and ideal sterile surgical environments need to be developed to ensure patient survivability. An increase in natural orifice procedures is also needed to perform surgeries through the mouth or anus. Enhanced transplants need to be developed to create healthier lives without the risk of complications. Better vaccines are required to combat diseases that are now threatening human beings in a deadly manner. More research is needed to create stronger antibiotics and antivirals that prevent the spread of communicable diseases. The development of enhanced imaging techniques and apparatuses will allow the viewing of bodies at a microscopic level to detect tumors, injuries and other maladies that cannot be seen with existing equipment. Better bionic inventions should be pursued to create more natural functioning, especially for arms, hands, legs and feet that have suffered amputations.

Genomic medicine can make patient-tailored therapies possible by improved molecular characterization of disease because human genetic variation is associated with many diseases and questions. New advances in technology that allow for quick and affordable genotypic assessments will lead to the understanding of the implications of human genetic variation for the treatment of disease. These patient-tailored therapies hold great promise as a new way of treating, or preventing, disease and significant investment must be made in this area of research. The effort should be one of lowering the cost of sequencing an individual's entire genomic sequence. Otherwise, we will not move away from the traditional medicine methodology of diagnosis based on clinical criteria, treatment that is population-based, and prevention that is based on late-stage identification of disease. Miniaturized diagnostic systems through the use of nanotechnology is another viable endeavor.

The direct administration of drugs to the respiratory tract can be used to treat bacterial lung infections, cystic fibrosis, and lung carcinoma. This injection-free way offers ways to control pain and deliver various therapeutics for the treatment of diabetes, human growth hormone deficiency and prostate cancer.

# Mining

Mining innovations are required to acquire the growing demand for mineral resources while at the same time protecting the environment. Smarter exploration, more efficient mining, safer working conditions to deal with inhospitable conditions or unknown dangers, and environmental solutions to deal with mine drainage, tailings and other environmental impacts are needed for the immediate future as mining transitions to a low-carbon economy.

Typical underground exploration is initially done through drilling. However, computer modeling and geological statistical software can be used to accelerate deposit discoveries. Innovation in this area can lead to less damaging aspects by pinpointing the exact locations of these deposits. Underground ore is usually extracted through the use of shafts, ramps, lighting and ventilation equipment, and horizontal and vertical tunnels. However, by the use of completely mechanized techniques it will be possible to extract large amounts of ores without exposing mineworkers to extremely hazardous conditions. Advances in electrolytic and flotation processes can be used to separate minerals in more purified forms. Rehabilitation is a necessary process to remove or neutralize contaminants from mine sites to restore the landscapes and minimize the geochemical impacts. Companies will need to venture into frontier mining areas.

As mining companies try to limit risk, novel financing will be needed to perform geographic information systems analyses, to create software programs and 3-D models to predict the location of deposits, and to conduct better gas sampling in potential ore deposit regions. Using geochemistry analyses to detect metals in surface materials and to predict the presence of underlying ore bodies by using GPS systems will better determine the ore locations. Conducting gravity studies and electromagnetic wave technology to pinpoint heavier ore locations, and using satellites to observe vast tracts of land that may not be readily accessible by land can also enhance mining techniques. Using seismic studies instead of explosions, spectrometry to analyze substances, geological metallurgy to determine optimal characteristics for processing ore, improved imaging techniques with inspection cameras, computerized density measurements, and using integrated development models before constructing a mine are all methods that can improve mining operations. New production models will be needed for the companies that do mining.

Better ventilation drilling, using polymer ducts and shaft liners, attachment of warning probes to detect possible cave-in conditions, wireless technology to provide better communication systems, gas-detection devices, wire mesh screens to retain rocks, more powerful LED headlamps with longer battery life, the manufacturing of sophisticated miner garments, fatigue measurement devices, the design of better escape capsules and survival chambers, and the use of robots and tele-mining can dramatically increase miner safety. Virtual training systems and mining simulators can be used to better prepare workers by exposing them to situations that they are likely to encounter—instead of directly exposing them to the real dangers of mine operations. New trucks that use lower fuel and oil consumption are needed to create less pollution as well as to provide vehicles that can drive on existing road infrastructures.

# Fire Fighting

Technological advances in firefighting are becoming critical as global warming occurs. This is particularly relevant in combating wildfires, which are becoming more prevalent. New thermal imaging cameras, fire surveillance drones, improved wind models, better fire shelters, creating more precise drops of water and fire retardant substances, and training with virtual reality are all methods that can improve the current situation. Improvements in personnel protective equipment must also be undertaken. This includes new types of self-breathing apparatus, high-tech fabrics for protective clothing, and personal alert safety system devices.

Fighting fire in buildings is a critical subject, especially with the advent of storage of new types of chemicals, gases and other flammable or explosive materials. Better sprinkler systems, water flow detectors, laser smoke detection systems, integrated pull alarms, voice evacuation systems and waterless suppression systems must be developed to better protect fire fighters, especially in warehouses and other storage buildings. Firehouses also need to be upgraded with a list that includes more powerful trucks, flexible ladder systems, portable and lightweight cutting tools, high-tech hoses, extrication gear, fire rescue tools, new types of foam and suppressants, and higher quality helmets. More powerful communication devices and monitors need to be developed to provide better coordination and safety in intensive fire situations, in particular, those that occur in high-rise buildings, which are being built in every city in the United States. Most cities are strapped for cash and cannot provide the necessary funds. It is the government that must take the lead in research, and in providing funds to better equip fire fighters who risk their lives for all us.

# Oceanography

Deep-water exploration needs to be conducted to discover the basic functioning of the oceans. But, more importantly, ocean surface effects need to be studied in greater detail to determine the effects of global warming as rises in sea levels and increases in global surface temperatures will affect the Pacific and Atlantic Oceans as well as the Gulf Coast. Very powerful impacts on the network of sea creatures and aquatic plants will affect people's lives in unpredictable ways. Mussels, crabs, clams, oysters will be severely impacted as salinity levels rise due to greater evaporation cycles caused by global warming.

Ocean acidification research requires more money to be spent to discover the adverse effects of fossil fuels and carbon dioxide on marine life. Support for ocean health and ocean management needs more funding to examine the effects of overfishing. Climate change needs to be studied in more detail to find out its effect in producing fiercer storms. Restoration is another area that could use more funding, especially in combatting the after effects of oil spills. Weather forecast models should also be expanded to provide more advance warnings for hurricanes.

Of particular importance is funding to combat marine pollution, which is threatening the oceans. The uncontrolled dumping of trash is creating several dead zones in the oceans where no life can exist. In addition, toxic spills and oil spills have produced devastating effects by affecting the food chain, and by creating dead zones where oxygen has been deprived. Research into biodegradable substances is important to prevent plastics and other non-soluble materials from being ingested by marine life. It is very critical in terms of its effects on food supplies since the decimation of swordfish, marlins, tuna, cod and halibut will create shortages that will be detrimental to human beings.

**Political Issues**

## Voting Methodology

The voting methodologies in the United States are obsolete. Currently, in many areas, counting is done with paper slips placed in popcorn containers and then sifted by hand—a process that is completely antiquated and which needs to be replaced. Electronic machines that are touch activated, computer-based voting that is done through the Internet, and database recording of all votes with appropriate backups, paper trails and storage are three ways in which the voting process can be updated. People don't need to stand in line for hours, sometimes in bad weather conditions, just to register a vote.

Our democracy depends on the strict and proper administration of election results. All voters must have assurance that their intent was correctly registered, and that all eligible votes were correctly tallied. Cryptographic techniques for implementing verifiable, secret ballot elections need to be fully explored. This is necessary because the mere installation of electronic voting machines or the implementation of Internet access voting is insufficient to achieve verification, secrecy and fraud prevention. Ways are needed to prevent fraud by means of tampering with machines, or by programming viruses or techniques that alter voting results stored in databases. Government funds need to be provided since most communities in the United States cannot afford the tasks that are necessary to achieve these new voting systems.

A database system, such as one that is based on Oracle software, that can be accessed through the Internet offers the best possibilities for secure voting. Each state can be made independent so that nationwide tampering is prevented. Only the final tabulations of each state can be made available for a national count. An Oracle database system also provides a nationwide analyses of voting patterns, demographics and other important data.

# Health Care

Although most developed countries have systems of socialized medicine, it is not a recommended solution for the United States. In spite of problems with having uninsured people, the United States still has the best system of medical care in the world. This is due to the profit motive that provides the incentive for innovations and for attracting the most qualified physicians with high-paying salaries. While a socialized system will cover the uninsured, it will detract from the economic situation with high taxation and untold bureaucracy.

Rising health care costs and one-size-fits-all solutions have led to limited, expensive options for consumers. Millions of Americans can no longer afford adequate care, or are forced to choose between providing health insurance for themselves and their families, or spending on necessities such as food, housing and utilities. The ACA offers a way to obtain insurance with coverage for existing solutions. However, it is constantly being challenged and underfunded, with the main objection being the required mandate that is attached to it. There are also concerns about health insurance being administered by the government.

Health care must be affordable, with a variety of consumer choices. Presently, health care costs too much, and leaves many people uninsured. The high insurance costs cut into workers' wages, as well as public budgets, and the employers' costs. Most families are vulnerable since a single medical emergency can lead to bankruptcy. Health care costs are the main financial concern for American families. In spite of the very high health costs, the United States has a higher infant mortality rate as well as a lower life expectancy as compared to other developed countries. Low-income people and the homeless have zero options, and they rely on home remedies and self -medication.

A prime factor in high health costs is with regard to very expensive drug costs that are charged by pharmaceutical companies. Prescription medicines are much higher in the United States that in other developed countries—even for generic drugs. This is particularly true for drugs that are used to combat cancer, HIV and other serious or complicated diseases.

There is no easy solution to the problem. Fixing doctors' fees through legislation will only result in less quality and quantity of skilled physicians. Fixing drug prices by law will end up with lower quality medications, with contrived shortages. The United States relies largely on a direct-fee system of private health care providers in which patients are expected to pay for medical costs themselves, aided by private health insurance, which is usually through one's employer. But, without some sort of competition, physicians, hospitals, and health care professionals and business are relatively free to charge whatever they want for their services.

Military personnel, Congressional members and the executive branch are covered by government-funded programs. Seniors over 65 years of age are covered by Medicare and by supplemental programs that are designed to cover the costs that Medicare does not completely cover. Special needs people are covered by Medicaid, special Social Security programs and by SCHIP. But, this is only a small portion of the population.

The lack of health insurance has deadly consequences because people that don't have it are less likely to receive preventive health care as well as care for various conditions and illnesses. Uninsured Americans are less likely to receive cancer screenings, and they are more likely to be diagnosed with more advanced cancers that often lead to death. Low-cost health insurance plans will not cover many types of illnesses and usually expire within a short period of time. Even policies that are bought without employee contributions result in hundreds or thousands of dollars in premiums, deductibles, coinsurance, and copayments.

Much of the cost of health insurance is directly due to the associated administrative costs for billing, record keeping, the required paperwork to apply it, and the many employees that are needed to do the accounting. Much of these costs could be greatly reduced with a streamlined electronic computer system to take advantage of database technologies that would make them more efficient. This database tracking system can also provide aggregate data on types of disease, age group vulnerabilities, recovery rates and performance statistics.

One development in coverage has been the rise of health maintenance organizations (HMOs). These plans enroll their subscribers through their workplaces. HMOs are prepaid health plans with designated providers, meaning that patients must visit a physician employed by the HMO or who are included on the HMO's approved list of physicians. However, if their physician is not approved by the HMO, then they have to either see an approved physician, or else see their own physician without insurance coverage. In some HMOs, patients have no guarantee that they can see the same physician at every visit. Instead, they see a physician that is assigned to them at each visit. This practice prevents physicians and patients from getting to know each other, it reduces the patients' trust in their physician, and may impair patient health due to the lack of shared patient condition knowledge.

A hidden problem in the medical practice is the apparent racial and gender bias in health care. Racial bias seems fairly common as African-Americans are less likely than whites with the same health problems to receive various medical procedures. There is also the impact of electronic health records based on racial and ethnic disparities in blood pressure control at primary care visits. Also, women are less likely than men with similar health problems to be recommended for various procedures, medications, and diagnostic tests, including cardiac catheterization, lipid-lowering medication, kidney dialysis, transplants, and knee replacement for osteoarthritis.

Other problems in the health care system are as follows:

- Sleep deprivation among health care professionals due to overworked hours and overloaded schedules, which can lead to errors in surgical procedures or mistakes in prescription dosages or types of medicines

- Shortages of physicians and nurses, especially in hospital emergency rooms, and in rural areas
- Mistakes or lack of strict procedures by hospitals such as making wrong diagnosis, being given the wrong drug, having a procedure done that was intended for someone else, or incurring a bacterial infection through lack of sanitation
- Medical fraud practiced by unscrupulous physicians, dentists, medical equipment companies, and nursing homes
- Medical ethics issues such as asking patients to take part in drug trials that might not be good for them just to earn additional money

A Medicare-for-all system sounds like a panacea, but it would entail a very high cost, probably in the trillions of dollars. The Medicare system is already very expensive to maintain, and adds immensely to the national debt. Taxing the rich to provide health care benefits to the poor will destroy the incentives for entrepreneurs if their money is taken away. Nevertheless, some sort of taxation will be required to provide health care benefits to those who cannot afford them.

In terms of prescription drug prices, there are better choices than enacting government price controls, which will inhibit access to new cures in the future, and that will cost hundreds of thousands of Americans to lose their jobs. Instead, legislation should be passed to do the following:

- Rework and reform the Medicare Part D benefit design.
- Facilitate the approval of generics and biosimilars.
- Help reduce costs for all Americans by moving towards a more value-based system that rewards outcomes and limits costs.
- Help Americans with out-of-pocket costs through expansion of Health Savings Accounts and Health Reimbursement Arrangements.
- Expand coverage options through mechanisms like Association Health Plans.
- Solidify the ACA's exchanges through the funding of cost-sharing reduction payments.

## Legalization of Marijuana

The United States federal government currently bans marijuana in a similar manner as it did for alcohol during Prohibition. The marijuana drug is extracted from the leaves of the hemp plant and is used for recreation, and to help people who are suffering from pain—such as from cancer, AIDS, multiple sclerosis, and neuropathic ailments. Forty states have decriminalized marijuana by passing laws controlling its sale, with some allowing doctors to prescribe it as a medicinal aid. However, the United States federal law does not agree with these state laws, and prosecutes people who use marijuana—using the federal Drug Enforcement Agency (DEA) as the policing arm.

In 2005, in the case of *Gonzalez v. Raich*, the Supreme Court ruled that under the Commerce Clause of the Constitution—which allows Congress to regulate commerce among the several states—Congress may ban homegrown cannabis, even where states have approved its use for medicinal purposes. The Supreme Court reasoned that banning the growing of marijuana for medical use was a permissible way of preventing or limiting access to marijuana for other uses.

In 2007, the Ninth Circuit Court decided against Angel Raich, when she renewed her litigation on substantive due process grounds. The case involved Angel Raich from Oakland, California who used homegrown medical marijuana, which is legal under California law, but illegal under federal law. Judge Harry Pregerson noted that while states have legalized medical marijuana, it is not a recognized fundamental right under the Due Process Clause of the Constitution. However, he also wrote that Reich could use medical necessity individually if she was ever arrested for using medical marijuana. In 2009, the DOJ issued new guidelines allowing for non-enforcement of the federal ban in some situations by stating that it will not be a priority to use federal resources to prosecute patients with serious illnesses or their caregivers who are complying with state laws on medical marijuana, but that the United States will still not tolerate drug traffickers who hide behind claims of compliance with state law to mask activities that are illegal.

More than one-half of all Americans under the age of 50 have tried marijuana, and at least 10% of American adults use the drug every year. However, the country's war on drugs places great emphasis on arresting people for smoking marijuana. During the period between 2000 and 2010, more than 6,500,000 Americans were arrested on marijuana charges. The total number of marijuana arrests exceeded the combined number of arrests for violent crimes—including murder, manslaughter, forcible rape, robbery and aggravated assault. Citizens who use marijuana are being arrested and treated like criminals because of the federal prohibition of marijuana. Hence, there is a push to decriminalize the use of marijuana at the federal level, with the basis being the Fourth and Fifth Amendments to the Constitution.

What is needed is probably another Amendment similar to the Twenty-First Amendment that lifted the federal restriction against alcoholic drinks, which had been instituted by the Eighteenth Amendment. All of the people that are currently in prison for having violated federal marijuana laws must be set free—except for big-time drug dealers.  With 80% of the states now having some sort of marijuana legalization, the enforcement of federal laws against marijuana is at odds with the prevailing social thinking.

# Women's Rights

Women's rights are the rights and entitlements that are claimed for women, and which formed the basis for the women's rights movement in the 19th century and the feminist movement during the 20th century. Issues that are commonly associated with notions of women's rights include the right to bodily autonomy, to be free from sexual violence, to have equal rights in law, to work for fair wages or equal pay, and to have reproductive rights.

Much has been done to advance women's rights since women gained the right to vote in the United States in 1920 via the Nineteenth Amendment. But, more needs to be accomplished, especially equal treatment under the law, reproductive rights, and employment rights. A key issue towards insuring gender equality in the workplace is the respecting of maternity rights and reproductive rights of women. Maternity leave as a temporary period of absence from employment should be granted immediately before and after childbirth to support the mother's full recovery and to grant time to care for the baby. Treating women and men alike does not work because certain biological aspects such as menstruation, pregnancy, labor, childbirth, breastfeeding, and certain medical conditions only affect women. The right to education for women is also affected by discrimination that nullifies or impairs equality of treatment in education. Academic education must include non-discrimination, ethics and gender equality for social advancement to be possible.

Women's health is severely impaired due to factors such as inequality, confinement of women to the home, indifference of medical workers, lack of autonomy of women, and lack of financial resources of women. Discrimination against women occurs through the denial of medical services that are only needed by women. Also, young women are the population most affected by HIV/AIDS and sexually transmitted infections.

The greatest struggle for women's emancipation is with respect to contraception and reproduction. This includes the right to legal or safe abortion, the right to control one's reproductive functions, the right to access quality reproductive health care, and the right to education and access to make reproductive choices free from coercion, discrimination and violence. Birth control has created a conflict between liberal and conservative values, raising questions about family, personal freedom, state intervention, religion in politics, sexual morality and social welfare. Abortion laws that restrict create situations of limited access to safe abortion services. In some areas, abortion is permitted only to save the pregnant woman's life, or if the pregnancy resulted from rape or incest. Forced sterilizations, forced pregnancies, denial or delay of post abortion care, abuse and mistreatment of women and girls seeking sexual and reproductive health information, goods and services, are all forms of gender based violence that amount to torture, cruel, inhuman or degrading treatment,

The abuse of women during childbirth is a recently identified problem that is a basic violation of a woman's rights. Abuse during childbirth can be in the form of neglect, physical abuse and lack of respect during childbirth. This treatment has the effect of preventing women from seeking pre-natal care and using other less viable health care services.

Child marriage is another practice which is often connected to poverty and gender inequality, especially the marriage of young girls to much older men. Child marriage endangers the reproductive health of young girls, leading to an increased risk of complications in pregnancy or childbirth. Forced pregnancy and forced marriage, including by means of bride kidnapping, through rape, or as part of a program of breeding are all forms of reproductive coercion. The discrimination applies to marriage and divorce laws, and in particular to polygamous marriage, such as in the state of Utah.

Violent acts that are committed against women means that they are forced into a subordinate position. These include acts of physical, sexual, psychological or economic harm or suffering to women, including threats of such acts, coercion or arbitrary deprivation of liberty, whether occurring in public or in private life. The violence against women may be perpetrated by individuals, by groups, by the State, or even by religious beliefs that condone "honor killings". Sexual exploitation is also an issue in which trafficking of women, prostitution and sex slaves exist.

Under male-dominated family law, women have had few, if any, rights, being under the control of the husband or male relatives. Legal concepts that have existed such as coverture and marital power have kept women under the strict control of their husbands. Restrictions from marriage laws have also extended to public life.

Discrimination against women is done by any distinction, exclusion or restriction made on the basis of sex which has the effect or purpose of impairing or nullifying the recognition, enjoyment or exercise by women, irrespective of their marital status, on a basis of equality of men and women, of human rights and fundamental freedoms in the political, economic, social, cultural, civil or any other field. The remedy is to put an end to sex-based discrimination, such as by the Equal Rights Amendment, for which states ratifying the Convention are required to enshrine gender equality into their domestic legislation, repeal all discriminatory provisions in their laws, and enact new provisions to guard against discrimination against women. The states must also establish tribunals and public institutions to guarantee women effective protection against discrimination, and take steps to eliminate all forms of discrimination practiced against women by individuals, organizations, and enterprises. All of these issues must be addressed to ensure true equality for women.

# Education

Funding for education is badly needed to provide the skills and knowledge for the new jobs that will be created. This includes grants for universities, student work-study programs, high school enhancement programs, grade school environment enrichment, new school construction, funding for more teachers and tuition funding. Better tracking of student behavior is badly needed for greater classroom security to prevent tragedies such as mass shootings.

Cloud-based learning platforms to improve access to instruction, mobile learning for complete online access to knowledge content, the application of gaming technologies, and other Internet innovations will greatly enhance education, especially for specific work skills that will be required in the future, and the creation of enriched learning environments to develop critical thinking and independent analyses. Learning through books and antiquated classroom techniques are totally deficient methods, which unfortunately are being used throughout the nation—mostly because of inadequate funding. For it is the unbundling of knowledge content that has the potential to transform the culture of established educational institutions as the sole providers of education and as the only source for rewarding employment.

The lack of funds to pursue a college education is a critical issue. Although the provision of free schooling is a terrific idea, there must be a way to support institutes of higher learning while at the same time making it affordable for poor people to attend. At present universities are getting money through donations for sports teams, but these only serve to mostly support the athletic programs. There has to be a way to support all fields of education, with government grants and scholarships being a distinct possibility.

Education is gaining the instrument of knowledge that enables people to obtain mastery over technical skills—the necessary ingredients for any state economy to thrive. But, it also has another component, and that is the acquisition of intelligence that enables everyone to observe, perceive and to understand oneself and others. It is the basis of order, which itself is the basis of freedom. It is what enables us to solve problems and to meet challenges. It is also the process of questioning and counter questioning that enables the truth to be revealed.

## Defense

For over 250 years of its existence, the United States has been continually involved in wars—except for only 16 of those years. The United States is spending billions on war and defense, including the support of the wars in Afghanistan and Iraq. Wasting more money on weapons of mass destruction is pointless exercise since we already have enough weapons to destroy the entire human race. But, defense spending can still be done at a reasonable level to develop new technologies and systems for ships, tanks, aircraft, submarines, missiles, drones, sonar, radar and laser weapons.

In contrast to the $7 trillion that has been spent on the wars in Iraq and Afghanistan, the investment in the infrastructure of the nation would require about 1% of that amount. We have gotten very little out of the money that has been spent on those two wars, other than destruction, loss of lives, the rise of terror groups, the creation of two failed states, economic chaos and misery. The conflicts have expanded and escalated to other regions, including Syria, Libya, Somalia and Yemen—and may even spread to Iran and Israel. The only accomplishment is that United States special forces have eliminated three of the world's top terrorists: Osama bin Laden, the leader of Al-Qaeda, Al-Baghdadi, the leader of ISIS, and General Qasam Soleimani, the leader of the Iranian Revolutionary Guards.

The experience of violence in the 20th century is a reminder of the carnage that has occurred. It is estimated that 100 million human beings perished in wars between 1900 and 2000. Since 1945, $5 trillion has been spent on the development of nuclear weapons by the United States—an amount that could have rebuilt the entire infrastructure in the country, including homes, factories, roads, bridges, railways, airports and ship facilities. There are a number of areas in which investments can produce a great amount of innovations that can stimulate the economy in contrast to huge expenditures on wars and defense.

After thousands of years we still believe that our political goals are only achieved by means of war. If the best that we can do is to bomb innocent civilians, and to coerce others with military and economic power, then there is no hope for humanity, and our children and grandchildren will be relegated to suffer the consequences of our actions. If the depravity, barbarism, corruption, violence and mayhem continue and become worse, then you will have to wonder where humanity is heading—especially if it all becomes driven by money and power without regard to any human values. The insanity of it is that the men and women that fight these wars get killed—or worse, get maimed and then are treated like broken toys. The human spirit gets crushed by war by all the insane actions of those who are committed to violence.

Wasting more money on weapons of mass destruction is absurd since we already have enough weapons to destroy the entire human race. While we don't need more nuclear weapons, we still need conventional arms to protect ourselves from hostile forces. Thus, we need military funds to be spent on ships, tanks, aircraft, submarines, missiles, drones, laser weapons, sonar weapons, and assault weapons. We also need to invest to protect soldiers with the provision of better bullet-proof vests, protective headgear, night-vision systems that provide enhanced details, portable surveillance systems, and increased protection of arms, hands, legs and feet. Better techniques and systems for the detection of atomic, biological and chemical agents also need to be developed.

Missile technology needs to be concentrated at the small type for perimeter defenses. Faster and sleeker ships such as destroyers should be constructed to provide a rapid deployment force. Aircraft carriers are fine, but they represent big targets that can be readily taken out with a missile. It is better to invest in more advanced submarines to protect the nation with incredible lethal armament arrays. Faster and more lethal aircraft need to be developed to provide a rapid deployment of forces wherever they are needed. Better, faster and more lethal drones are a requirement to better fight small battles. Drones also need to be equipped with AI technology to provide greater flexibility in guidance for targeting.

Laser weapons are a definite must. This is in contrast to anti-ICBM missile systems that are extremely expensive to develop and, which at best only provide a 60% coverage against incoming missiles. Only very powerful laser weapons can deal with incoming missile threats by zapping them before they do any damage. Smaller laser weapons that can be mounted on land vehicles and on ships also need to be developed to destroy rockets, artillery, mortars and drones. More lethal assault weapons and associated ammunition are also required for foot soldiers.

## Intelligence Gathering

Agencies such as the FBI, CIA, DNI and NSA collect all types of data for the purpose of obtaining security for the United States. While this is an essential activity, there needs to be a tighter control on the activities of these agencies to ensure that personal liberties are not at risk by the conduction of clandestine activities. Intelligence gathering can provide several kinds of information. It can provide observations during travel or other events from travelers, refugees, and escaped friendly prisoners. It can provide data on things about which the subject has specific knowledge, which can be another human subject, or, in the case of defectors and spies, sensitive information to which they had access. It can also provide information on interpersonal relationships and networks of interest.

In terms of dealing with terrorists, we should not continue to rely on inhumane interrogation techniques that involve torture. sleep deprivation, isolation or the creation of helplessness in captive individuals. Sources of information may be neutral, friendly, or hostile, and may or may not be witting of their involvement in the collection of information. Properly recording and cross-indexing the results of interviews with these individuals is essential to prevent any abuses. It is also important during interrogations to build a relationship with the subject, a relationship that can be based on trust, friendship, or any of a range of positive human emotions. Prisoners have an understandable fear of what may happen, and it can be important to relax them and, as much as possible, put them at ease.

Good information gathering requires well-trained professionals who can also speak foreign languages. More advanced surveillance equipment is also necessary to obtain phone and vocal conversations, to get visual data of activities and individuals, and excellent camera and video equipment to be able to track movements of people and vehicles. While companies can develop the surveillance tools, it is the government that must fund the research to develop these technologies.

# Economic Factors

# Financial Systems

Financial systems are at the heart of the economy and include banks, mortgage institutions, financial companies and the stock market. Financial management software must undergo a major transformation, especially with respect to in-memory database technology and multi-tenant cloud computing. Modern financial applications can leverage these approaches to challenge the traditional architectures of finance systems, especially for financial reporting and analytics. Quicker access for users to access financial data necessitates a much greater level of data granularity across multiple business dimensions is also required. A multi-tenant model will use cloud-computing applications, to deliver data to the entire customer community at the same time., and new data will be delivered in the cloud as soon as it becomes available.

Mobile banking has become the norm for customer touch point banking services. But, mobile banking has increased fivefold in a very short period of time. This growth will see a shift in mobile banking operations as they continue to add more functionalities and newer features in their mobile banking solutions. The personal finance management tools (PFM) are now being placed in a prominent place in the online banking sites so that customers get to know what new services are available. Regional banks are also trying to make PFM online work in tandem. The introduction of message centers on a widespread basis is needed for this. These are dedicated web portals that are designed for secure communication between a bank and its customers. Tablet banking requires upgrades to allow transactions such as remote deposit captures.

In terms of mortgages, links in the chain that have traditionally been bottlenecks will have to be addressed further upstream in the origination process, especially because speed is a critical element of financial success. Less paperwork will be generated as digitization becomes more prevalent. New digital tools will enable people to apply directly for mortgages—without all of the cumbersome paperwork and legal forms that are now required to be filled out. The tracking of mortgages will be simplified so that less "red tape" will be involved while providing more transparency.

Stock market trading needs refinements in algorithmic and automated trading software, especially those that limit the velocity at which share prices fall before a halt is called to trading in a particular stock. The stock market needs to be able to provide sufficient latency to support more regular and faster trading to allow investors to take market opportunities more quickly. The lowering of transaction costs with faster access will also mean huge volume increases in transactions. Innovations of speed are necessary to take care of the increased volumes, and to provide algorithmic trading and flexibility that will integrate trading across asset classes and across markets.

Many public companies now publicize business and financial information on the Internet, but few of them use the Internet or other electronic media to meet delivery and disclosure requirements under the federal securities laws. Investment companies are electronically providing a substantial amount of information and services to a large number of investors via the Internet. Investors are taking advantage of the enormous amount of information that is available electronically from investment companies, and are making additional demands for increased electronic information flow. New computer technologies, and increasing access to the Internet have the potential to affect investment advisory services.

Brokers, dealers and institutional investors are now using powerful computer systems and sophisticated applications to manage inventory, order flow and risk, and to receive market data, research reports and company information electronically. However, because the Internet provides an easy method for cross-border communications, abuses of the Internet emphasize the need for coordinated activities with foreign securities regulators. Electronic access to shareholder meetings and corporate communications must be implemented to provide greater transparency for the individual investors.

While many mutual funds have used electronic media to be more accessible to the average investor, many investors have used electronic media to transform themselves into more sophisticated and well-educated consumers. Many third parties have recognized the importance of investment companies in the economy, and have developed information services that are tailored specifically for investment company investors. These third parties have also made extensive use of electronic media to reach investors, adding to the amount of information readily available.

More is required to be done, especially with regard to regulation and security. This includes the availability of disclosure documents, private offerings, and other shareholder information. This is particularly true for retirement investing. There are many uses for new interactive technologies in the administration of contribution plans in uncomplicated ways for employees to receive account balances. All of these are areas that private companies and the SEC must invest in new technologies to create a sounder, less-risky and more inclusive stock trading environment complete with advisory services and surveillance, especially with regard to OTC transactions, derivatives and bond markets. Every effort must be made to prevent fraudulent securities offerings, market manipulations and disclosure failures.

The one huge financial issue that looms large for the United States concerns the national debt. With the figure now at almost $24 trillion—an amount equal to $72,000 for every person in the United States—it is difficult to see how this will ever be significantly reduced, especially since federal spending keeps increasing. President George W. Bush contributed $6 trillion of that amount, President Barack Obama contributed $8.5 trillion, and President Donald Trump has already contributed $9.5 trillion. *Because of other liabilities such as Medicaid, Medicare and Social Security, the real level of total debt is about $75 trillion—a figure of over $225,000 per person!*

# Home Building

With global warming increasing, more homebuyers are demanding green homes, and home builders are looking for cost-effective, sustainable ways to deliver them. Recent advances in green building technologies are bringing carbon-neutral and zero net-energy homes closer to reality. Some of these innovations are with zero-carbon and zero net-energy homes, solar power, grid-aware appliances, hydrocarbon refrigerants, on-site water treatment, myco form building blocks, new types of flooring, intelligent window design, and by increasing urban density.

Zero-carbon and zero net-energy homes use only as much energy as they can produce. Zero-carbon homes use no fossil fuels and produce no greenhouse gasses. To achieve carbon neutrality or zero net-carbon homes, builders must employ a number of techniques, such as external walls that are made of thick, insulated concrete to protect interiors from temperature fluctuations. Geothermal wells capture water warmed by rooftop solar panels and circulate it through radiant heated floor systems or closed-loop cooling systems. Roofs may also be V-shaped to collect water.

Solar technology has limitations. To achieve maximum efficiency, solar cells must be pointed directly at the sun. Unless they are mounted on mechanical tracking devices, solar panels are only able to operate at maximum efficiency for a few hours each day. A new breakthrough that creates spherical micro solar cells, which can absorb light from any direction, including light reflected off other surfaces needs to be implemented in all future solar homes for maximum efficiency.

Appliance manufacturers are currently bringing grid-smart washer/dryers, refrigerators, televisions, thermostats, hot water heaters and other appliances to market. The ability of these machines to measure and monitor their own use is at the heart of zero-carbon and zero net-energy home building. Replacing HFC refrigerants with hydrocarbon refrigerants will be required because they have a much lower potential for global warming.

The process of collecting, treating and reusing water that's not considered drinkable, but might be suitable for other activities, is an innovation in home building. By diverting drainpipes into collection tanks, homeowners can capture rainwater, snowmelt and the water that drains away after showering, washing dishes or laundering clothes. The water in these collection tanks is filtered and reused for flushing toilets, irrigating landscapes and cycling through closed-loop radiant heating and cooling systems.

Many houses have been built from recycled materials. However, building materials can be created from brick molds made from recycled aluminum sheets that grow mycelium spores inside the form. New types of tiles can create resilient floors, and smart windows that are treated with ultrahigh tech nano coatings can be as energy-efficient as walls.

Another technique in home building is by increasing urban density. Putting more people into less space promotes communities that are promote walking, and are thus less dependent upon vehicles. People don't have to live on top of each other in high-rise condominiums to create urban density. Sustainable, spacious, multifamily and mixed-use developments with retail stores on the street level and residential units above can be built through modern architectural structures. Investment in newer home building technologies can produce 3D printed houses, disaster relief houses, open space habitats and other planned urbanization. Both industry and government must pursue research into these areas of home building.

## Transportation

Great strides can be accomplished in the field of transportation. New types of aircraft, trains, buses, subways, automobiles and trucks need to be developed that are more energy efficient and less polluting. Electric cars offer a great alternative to gas-powered automobiles. More money needs to be allocated for battery research to create more powerful vehicles that have greater ranges before recharging is required. Hybrid vehicles offer new possibilities, especially by using less-polluting fuels.

Intelligent transportation systems will make driving safer by providing better techniques for traffic management. But most cities lack funds with which to implement even fundamental systems. Research into alternative fuels must be greatly accelerated to curb the rise of toxic hydrocarbons into the atmosphere. Coordinating traffic signals, giving signal priority to transit lanes, electronic information signs and variable speed limit signs are also necessary to distribute real-time traffic data to websites, mobile apps, and local communication facilities. This is particularly germane to connected vehicles that rely on wireless networks to control speed, heading and direction. Self-driving cars that do not require driver input offer a new system of safe transportation on roadways. But, without making investments in transportation technology, the problems of congestion, pollution and more accidents will only make things more difficult and costly.

# Infrastructure

The infrastructure in the United States is crumbling. There is an urgent need to rebuild or at least refurbish bridges, roads, inland waterways and tunnels. Underground power delivery systems need to be done to prevent the massive power outages that are currently experienced when power lines go down due to high winds. Water distribution systems need to be upgraded to prevent a disaster such as the one that occurred in Flint, Michigan. The funding that is required to create a more viable infrastructure in the United States is indeed very great—but it must be done, or else we will decay into a third-world country.

Decaying infrastructure can be found all across the United States. Structurally deficient unsafe bridges, overflowing sewage drains, urban traffic congestion caused by lack of more roads, outdated air traffic control systems that create dangers for airplanes, seaports that are becoming obsolete, and roads that are filled with potholes and other hazards—all of these are critical items that must be fixed. And yet, *funding for infrastructure in the United States is now at its lowest point during the last 70 years*!

Thousands of deaths have occurred as a result of decaying infrastructure every year, especially because of unsafe highways and roads. Damaged pipelines that carry dangerous fuels such as natural gas run under the streets and buildings of almost every major American city, and a few of these have already blown up. Commercial air travel in America is being impacted by long security lines, delayed departures and missed connections due to outdated and overcrowded airports—a situation that can be remedied by building new flight hubs to relieve the burdens of the major airports in this country. The busiest rail lines have been repeatedly shut down by failing power cables. Many railway accidents have been experienced due to the lack of positive train control technology that can automatically slow down speeding rail traffic over dangerous curves. Crumbling beams and eroding concrete are present in thousands of bridges across the country.

The American people must decide what their tax dollars should be spent on. If their decision is not to spend for infrastructure repair and renewal, then a very huge price will be paid by all for the failure to spend on the urgently needed upgrade of the United States—*especially in the quality of life*. In this effort, the pursuing of tax cuts will spur limited economic growth and take money away from the investments that are essential to renew the infrastructure.

# Agriculture

While advances in agriculture have produced an abundant source of food for the United States, there are still areas that can be improved to produce a more viable system of food production. Air and soil sensors can be used to automate farms to provide real time conditions. Equipment telematics can be installed on farm vehicles to warn of imminent failures. Livestock biometric devices can be used to provide real time information. High-resolution crop sensors can inform accurate field fertilization before application. Optical sensors with infrared technology and drones can identify crop health. Infrastructural health sensors can be used to monitor conditions in buildings and other farm structures. Genetically designed food—rather than genetically modified food—can be used to create new strains of food animals and plants. In vitro meat (cultured meat) can be used to augment the supply of protein.

The use of variable rate swath control can save on seed, minerals, fertilizer and herbicides by reducing overlapping inputs. By pre-computing the shape of the field where the inputs are to be used, and by understanding the relative productivity of different areas of the field, tractors can apply inputs at variable rates throughout the field. The use of rapid iteration selective breeding can analyze the end-result so that improvements can be made for better crops. Agricultural robots can be used to automate agricultural processes, such as harvesting, fruit picking, plowing, soil maintenance, weeding, planting and irrigation.

With satellite imagery and advanced sensors, farmers can optimize returns on inputs while preserving resources. Further understanding of crop variability, geo-located weather data and precise sensors will allow improved automated decision-making and complementary planting techniques. The combination of agricultural robots with microscopic sensors can be used to monitor, predict, cultivate and extract crops from the land. Also, the use of closed ecological systems can transform waste products into oxygen, food and water to support crops and animals inhabiting the system.

Synthetic biology can be used to design, build and remediate engineered biological systems that process information, manipulate chemicals, fabricate materials and structures, produce energy, provide food, and maintain and enhance human health and our environment. Vertical farms can cultivate plant or animal life within upward structures. By using techniques that are similar to glass houses, vertical farms can augment natural light to create year-round crop production, protection from weather, as well as to support urban food autonomy and reduce transport costs.

All that is required for these innovations is an investment in the appropriate technologies. This is a very important area to focus on because it involves the survival of people as the population grows, which will continue to add pressures on food production and distribution systems.

## Drivers for Economics

Drivers for economics include housing financing, rural development and tax reform. A very important area of economic forecasting is to prevent disasters such as the Great Depression in 1929 and the Great Recession in 2008. Better models are needed to pinpoint and identify possible uncertainties to prevent or at least better manage economic declines. Real time forecasting needs to be improved through the use of supercomputers and better database storage of relevant information.

The removal of mortgage constraints and better access to credit are large factors in housing financing. The tendency for housing prices to continually rise requires a fix such as the provision of government housing for low-income families who are currently priced out of the market. Advances in rural development require priority attention to reverse poverty and deteriorating neighborhoods. It is a matter of putting human beings first to reduce the income and living conditions gap between the haves and the have-nots.

# Taxation

America's system of taxation is in need of reform. Currently, we have a relatively narrow corporate tax base—one that is reduced by tax loopholes and untaxed expenditures. The current tax system distorts choices, such as where to produce, what to invest in, and how to finance. It does little to encourage job creation and investment within the United States while allowing firms to benefit from incentives to locate production elsewhere and to shift taxable income and profits overseas.

This tax system only produces unemployment because of limited job opportunities. Eliminating loopholes and subsidies will broaden the tax base and will lower tax rates such that American manufacturing and innovation will be strengthened, with the retaining of jobs that would otherwise be lost to foreign firms. However, the tax reform needs to be done in a way that does not add to the national debt because tax revenues are needed to start paying off the massive debt. Tax reform should not only eliminate undesirable incentives, but it should also provide incentives to support economic activities that benefit the broader economy within the nation. Equitable taxation is a necessary implementation in the United States.

# Trade

Free trade is the preferable method of exchange of goods between countries and unions. Any tariffs or quotas that are imposed only serve to lessen trade by putting artificial barriers. The only people that get hurt are the consumers since they ultimately wind up paying the tariff fees since these are simply passed on by the corporations to the buyers of the goods. Of course, there must be a reasonable balance of trade existing between countries; otherwise, it is an unfair practice, which can be compounded by currency manipulations. But, protectionism, which restrains and discourages trade between nations has a negative effect upon free trade.

# Globalization

Globalization is a form of capitalist expansion which entails the integration of local and national economies into a global, unregulated market economy. Globalization has grown due to advances in transportation and communication technology. With the increased global interactions comes the growth of international trade, ideas, and culture. Globalization is primarily an economic process of interaction and integration that's associated with social and cultural aspects. However, conflicts and diplomacy are large parts of modern globalization.

Economically, globalization involves goods, services, the economic resources of capital, technology, and data. The expansions of global markets liberalize the economic activities of the exchange of goods and funds. Removal of trade barriers has made formation of global markets more feasible. Advances in the means of transport, the Internet and mobile phones have been part of the development in the telecommunications infrastructure. All of these improvements have generated further interdependence of economic and cultural activities around the globe that have impacted trade and transactions, capital and investment ventures, migration and movement of people, and which have greatly expanded the dissemination of knowledge.

In the 21st century, environmental challenges such as global warming, cross-boundary water, air pollution, and over-fishing of the ocean are all affecting globalization. Globalization is being affected by business and work organizations, economic systems, religious, social and cultural differences, politics, and the natural environment. America's policies should be geared towards greater globalization since this will enhance the economy. Going the route of "America First" only generates negative effects because it creates an environment that is no longer conducive to the free exchange of trade, data and technology.

# Unemployment

Unemployment and the status of the economy can be influenced by fiscal and monetary policy. Unemployment can be affected by the introduction of new technologies and inventions, especially those of robotics that can displace human workers. Unemployment can also be influenced by recessions that contract spending, and cause companies to lay off workers as they cut back on production. Competition due to globalization and international trade are two more factors that affect unemployment. Restrictive regulation and excessive market control can affect unemployment as well.

Structural unemployment focuses on foundational problems in the economy and inefficiencies inherent in labor markets, including a mismatch between the supply and demand of laborers with necessary skill sets. Functional unemployment focuses on voluntary decisions to work based on each individuals' valuation of their own work and how that compares to current wage rates plus the time and effort required to find a job. Cyclical unemployment occurs when there is not enough aggregate demand in the economy to provide jobs for everyone who wants to work. Demand for most goods and services falls, less production and fewer workers are needed, and unemployment results. Involuntary unemployment is when a person is willing to work at the prevailing wage yet is not hired.

All of these unemployment possibilities can always be alleviated through government programs and allocations of monies for creating jobs. Industries can always provide jobs if they are given the incentives to do so. However, it is not enough to give tax cuts to the corporations because without some sort of agreement, they will just pocket the extra money that is obtained by tax cuts to produce bigger profits instead of investing it to create new jobs. The same is true for banks since they can increase their wealth instead of increasing their loans to businesses and persons.

Recessions are harder to deal with since they involve fiscal and monetary fixes. Decreasing interest rates only works so far before a point is reached that leads to negative interest rates, which becomes a liquidity trap. Printing extra money only works if enough jobs are created to offset the inflation that comes with an increase in money. It is a delicate balance.

# Automation

## Overview

Automation which uses various control systems for operating equipment such as machinery, processes in factories, boilers and heat treating ovens, switching on telephone networks, steering and stabilization of ships, aircraft and other applications and vehicles is done with minimal or reduced human intervention, thus requiring fewer workers. Automation has been achieved by various means including mechanical, hydraulic, pneumatic, electrical, electronic devices, robots and computers. The benefit of automation comes mostly from labor savings as well as by improvements to quality, accuracy, and precision, outweighing the economic effects of workers being displaced by automation. As a result of job losses and downward mobility blamed on automation, it has become a factor in the resurgence of protectionist politics in the United States.

## Advantages of Automation

The main advantage of automation is that it creates faster production and cheaper labor costs. Another benefit is that it replaces hard, physical, or monotonous work. Also, tasks that take place in hazardous environments or that are otherwise beyond human capabilities can be done by machines that can operate under extreme temperatures, in atmospheres that are toxic, or in areas that are dangerous, such as with radioactive materials. Automation performs tasks that are beyond human capabilities of size, weight, speed and endurance. Also, automated machines can be maintained with simple quality checks.

## Disadvantages of Automation

Not all tasks can be automated, and some tasks are more expensive to automate. Initial costs of installing the machinery in factory settings are high, and the failure to maintain a system could result in the loss of the product itself. There are also possible security threats and vulnerability due to increased relative susceptibility for committing

## Limitations to Automation

A current limitation is that technology is unable to automate all of the desired tasks. Many operations using automation have large amounts of invested capital and produce high volumes of product, making malfunctions extremely costly and potentially hazardous. Also, as a process becomes increasingly automated, there is less and less labor to be saved or quality improvement to be gained. As more processes become automated, there are fewer remaining non-automated processes, which leads to an exhaustion of opportunities.

Other limitations are processes that are presently beyond the scope of automation. These are processes such as human-level pattern recognition, language comprehension, and language production ability. Tasks requiring subjective assessment or synthesis of complex sensory data, such as scents and sounds, as well as high-level tasks such as strategic planning, currently require human expertise.

With automation, the more efficient the automated system becomes, the more crucial the human contribution of the operators becomes. Humans may be less involved, but their involvement becomes more critical because if an automated system has an error, it will multiply that error until it is fixed or shut down. This is where human operators come in. However, even where humans are available to intervene, the automated system can still override everything. Two fatal examples were the two Boeing 737 MAX jets, where a failure of guidance and control automation put the pilots into a situation that they were not prepared for, and the automatic system caused the two fatal crashes because pilots did not know how to disengage it.

## A Cause of Unemployment

Employees who are engaged in tasks that follow well-defined procedures that can easily be performed by sophisticated algorithms and machinery are most at risk of displacement. One-half of the jobs in the United States are at risk of replacement by automation., especially in putting low-paid physical occupations at risk. Increased automation causes workers to feel anxious about losing their jobs as technology renders their skills or experience unnecessary. Automation is already contributing significantly to unemployment in the United States, and one-half of current jobs have the potential to be fully automated by 2033. Prospects are particularly bleak for occupations that do not require a university degree.

While the number of jobs lost to automation is often offset by jobs gained from technological advances, the same type of job loss is not the same one replaced and that is leading to increasing unemployment in the lower-middle class. This occurs largely where technological advances contribute to higher demand for highly skilled labor but demand for middle-wage labor continues to fall.

Unemployment is becoming a problem in the United States due to the exponential growth rate of automation and technology. As many jobs are becoming obsolete, which is causing job displacement, one possible solution would be for the government to assist with a universal basic income program to provide displaced workers with extra money to spend on education and training on new demanding employment skills. But even the provision of a basic income doesn't address the issue of income inequality, which will be exacerbated by job displacement caused by automation.

**Social Issues**

# Substance Abuse

Many people in the United States have a substance addiction—substances that are harmful in the long run. In terms of substances that people ingest or inhale, there are three major categories that inflict major damage to bodies and minds: tobacco, alcohol and drugs. Enormous amounts of resources in terms of money, health practitioners and facilities need to be applied to make an effort at massive rehabilitation efforts.

## Tobacco

The use of tobacco leads to diseases that affect the heart and lungs, with smoking being a major risk for heart attacks, chronic pulmonary diseases like emphysema and cancer—particularly lung cancer, cancers of the larynx and mouth, and pancreatic cancer. Tobacco smoke also contains carcinogens that induce a secondary effect through exposure, and is definitely known to cause cancer in humans who may not have used tobacco products. The main effect of tobacco use is that it requires extensive medical facilities and extended doctor care to treat the victims.

Many types of treatment are available, including skin patches, chewing gum with additives and so forth. However, the main objective should be education so that young people do not start using tobacco products. The payoff is great since abstinence will reduce cancers, digestive diseases, lung ailments and heart disease—thus decreasing health costs, which will add to the economic well-being. As for those who are addicted already, the aim should be withdrawal so that they can regain their health and reduce medical costs that are associated with tobacco use.

## Alcohol

The abuse of alcohol can cause or worsen many medical problems—and can destroy families and lives. Alcohol abuse causes thousands of deaths each year, and is most commonly abused by children. Motor vehicle, airplane and boating accidents, engagement in high-risk sexual behaviors, low academic achievement, degraded job performance and psychological depression are some of the results of alcohol abuse.

Long-term heavy drinking damages the liver, stomach, esophagus, nervous system, heart, kidneys and brain. It can also lead to high blood pressure, intestinal problems, cancer and osteoporosis. Mentally, alcohol abuse can lead to violence, social isolation, incarceration, personality changes, blackouts and difficulties in thinking. The combination of alcohol with medicines or drugs may increase the effects of each in disproportion to their singular effects. In the end stages, alcoholism leads to symptoms such as trembling, delusions, hallucinations, and sweating. There is a high economic cost that is incurred in terms of medical facilities to treat alcohol abusers—as well as associated insurance costs.

Again, the main objective should be education so that young people do not start drinking at an early age. It will also help to inform young people about the effects of overdrinking. As for those who are alcoholics, the best treatment is withdrawal—with the benefit being better health and less medical services needed—both of which will enhance the economic well-being.

## Drugs

Drug abuse includes both prescription drugs such as morphine and opioids, partially legal drugs like marijuana, and illegal drugs—such as methamphetamines, cocaine, crack, heroin, hash, opium, ecstasy and LSD. Most people use drugs to get "high," to fit in, to experiment, or to relieve stress, boredom and emotional problems. Drug addiction results in overdoses that require emergency room treatments, with some of them even becoming victims of sexual assault or violent incidents because of uncontrolled behavior. The bad part of the drug problem is that it creates the conditions for crime and trafficking to flourish. The worst part is that it destroys the normal functioning of the brain of the person who is doing drugs—thereby reducing the capability of that person to thrive, to enjoy well-being, and to live with zest and aliveness.

Mind-altering drugs are dissociative and their interactions with the brain produce structural changes, some of which alter the neural pathways and functioning of vital connective tissues in the brain. The most insidious impairment that may result from prolonged ingestion of drugs is the destruction of the brain's ability of attention and concentration. The destructive damage can in turn lead to violent acts, the abolishment of all values, and the unearthing of hidden primal and instinctive behaviors. Besides causing the deterioration of the psyche and flesh, the use of drugs has very significant social effects and economic costs associated with them. With respect to drugs that are illegal, these create situations that breed crime—oftentimes with violent events wherever syndicates and cartels are involved in the trafficking of these substances.

Better education is required so that young people do not get lured into taking drugs. For those who are already addicted to drugs, withdrawal is the best course to follow. Better use of legal drugs is definitely a requirement since too many people are addicted to opioids and similar prescription drugs. The payoff is terrific in having people retreat from their drug-induced states of mind. All of this adds to the economic well-being of the country, as well as benefitting the social environment.

# Psychology and Psychiatry

Mental health issues have become very important in America, especially with the proliferation of guns. Counseling by psychologists and psychiatrists have not been effective enough to ensure the safety of others by deranged individuals. There is not enough known about the human psyche to prescribe the medications that are given out by health practitioners. More advances need to be made to ferret out individuals who pose harm to themselves and to others because when people feel lonely, their behavior and physiology are disrupted, creating a trap that reinforces their isolation—and possible derangement of behavior.

With the advent of modern neuroscience, the contributions that neurochemistry makes to psychological observations in human behavior are becoming clearer. When people are provided with proper therapy, which can include medications under the care of a well-trained therapist, they can make giant strides toward recovery. Yet, the environment has a large—and largely unrecognized—effect on people's behavior. Emotions also play a large role in behaviors, especially in decision-making. The point is that human beings are very complex organisms, and every aspect of modern life is touched by psychology. But, while mental health practitioners may know enough to treat some symptoms with proper medication, they cannot deal or treat the ultimate causes of aberrant behaviors. Genetics plays an important part by transmitting genes that are responsible for the heritability of many behavioral disorders that begin in childhood.

Molecular genetics is now able to identify some of the specific DNA variants that are responsible for this heritability. The genetic structure of common disorders differs significantly from diagnostic classifications based on symptoms. The interface between nature and nurture is also important in identifying influences that can lead to disorders of the mind since social context alters genetic expression. RNA plays an important role in the expression of DNA-based expressions. Individual genome sequencing needs to be done for every individual to have a basic set of data for every individual.

Psychological science needs to be integrated with other scientific disciplines. Some of the areas that might be beneficial for research into behaviors are as follows:

- Neuroscience—the use of magnetic resonance imaging to obtain brain scans, to monitor autonomic and neuroendocrine processes, and to make assays of immune function. More explorations are needed of neural mechanisms of emotion, cognitive behavior, and analyses of how the brain mediates social interactions. More studies are definitely required of how cultural values, practices, and beliefs mold the mind, brain, and genes.
- Behavioral economics—studies of how social and emotional factors influence economic decisions. Human judgment and financial decision-making are influenced greatly by financial uncertainty.
- Educational aspects—focuses on the interactions between biological processes and education. These are examinations of the neural mechanisms of reading, math comprehension, and attention, as well as learning disabilities such as

dyslexia and attention deficit disorder.
- False memory research—studies of how memory is fallible and highly suggestible. The psychological and legal aspects of distorted or false memories are that they are subject to contamination and manipulation. False memories can be triggered in individuals through the power of suggestion, which sometimes leads to false memories of abuse, molestation, and alien abduction—even if they appear to be very vivid memories. Imagining an event can lead to the later belief that it really happened, and may influence memory distortion in brain-damaged patients.
- Behavioral epigenetics—studies of infancy and how infants react to stress when they receive less care in their upbringing. These infants become more sensitive to stress throughout their lives, and result in modifications in brain tissue, particularly in the hippocampus, which is a brain region that regulates stress responses. Environmental factors can alter behavior by biochemically changing the function of genes or gene expression, especially among individuals who have been abused as children.
- Implicit association and bias—studies of unconscious and automatic thought processes. These are association traits such as implicit racism and other forms of bias. The presence of implicit bias in a variety of contexts exists everywhere, including with elections and in courtrooms. The impact that implicit biases have on behavior may be very strong.
- Stereotype threats—when people are confronted with negative stereotypes about one of their group identities such as age, social class, race, gender, religion, and so forth. These persons feel a pressure not to confirm to the stereotype, or not to be judged by it, which can undermine behaviors in the immediate situation, which may result in violent behaviors as a response to the inflicted stereotype.
- Human-computer interaction—largely the Internet's effect on individuals and groups. These include online relationships, addiction to multiplayer games, behavior in online social networks, and cyber bullying. There are also links between social networking use and narcissism, and virtual reality environments that can set off post-traumatic stress disorders. This is particularly true with the advent of new input techniques such as voice and gesture commands.
- Terrorism—the examination of the mindsets of ideological radicals. Joining terrorist groups may give individuals a sense of security and meaning that they may be missing in their lives. Research must be done to study the causes of radicalization as an effort towards reducing it.

# Prison Reform

Prisons are necessary in our society, but technological advances can make these institutions safer. Some of these innovations are as follows:

- Imaging systems and handheld scanners that make it easier to detect makeshift weapons like shivs and other improvised objects that inmates often fashion from plastic and metal. The identification of such weaponry makes jails safer.
- Needle-free injection systems for medicating and immunizing sick inmates. This makes the healthcare process safer for doctors and inmates, and prevents criminals from doing harm to others with needles.
- Electronic detection of cell phones hidden beneath floors and inside walls by detection of calls and text messages
- Radio frequency identification tracking to keep track of an inmate's or cell block's whereabouts. It saves guards time, and will change the way that prisons are run and prisoners are tracked.
- Biometric technology to detect a person by their retinas and fingerprints to allow prison officials to tell who and where inmates and employees are at all times
- Tasers for use in prison riots
- Tele-health camera-based systems to diagnose and deliver health services by using telecommunications technology. This will save lives of inmates and reduce costs of prisons.

Prison reform is necessary to prevent the increasing number of people who are in jail. Many of these are in prison because of marijuana-related offenses, something that is obviously hypocritical given that many states have legalized it. The criminal justice reform law that was passed by Congress in 2018 aims to give prisoners who exhibit good behavior the possibility to shorten their sentences, particularly for nonviolent drug offenses. The law attempts to curve recidivism, the rate at which convicted individuals engage in further criminal activity upon release. A second phase of this reform effort will be focused on the successful reentry of former inmates, which will reduce unemployment for Americans with past criminal records. More advanced DNA, fingerprinting and facial recognition techniques are also necessary to prevent the incarceration of innocent people.

## The Homeless Problem

Currently, there are over 2 million homeless persons in the United States according to advocates who work with the homeless. The population of individuals who are homeless is expected to triple over the next decade. In regards to the elderly, the impending wave of homeless seniors will come with an increase in aging-related health care costs. Homeless people are generally not given housing until they have solved or been treated for the problems that got them onto the streets, whether these problems are related to financial, health or addiction issues. Homeless shelters are a band aid, especially since homeless people will tend to accumulate health problems and wait until they end up in emergency hospitals or emergency psychiatric care, which is very expensive.

Throwing money at the homeless problem by itself will not alleviate the situation. Building shelters for them is a necessary task—but it must be done in a way that is responsible. Otherwise, all that will happen is a decay of these shelters into ghettos and slums. Areas must be set aside as communities for the homeless, with access to medical care, opportunities for employment, and with environments that induce good and healthy living conditions.

# Proliferation of Firearms

## Overview

The growing number of civilians holding firearms is fueling gun crime and is putting healthcare systems under stress, especially in poor areas. Shootings kill 30,000 people a year in the United States, and injures many more. The proliferation of civilian gun arsenals is not likely to slow anytime in the foreseeable future, especially since civilians are acquiring greater numbers of increasingly more powerful guns. The current estimate is that there are 393,000,000 guns in the United States, ranging from handguns to assault rifles. This figure represents more than the number of people in the United States.

## Causes

The failure of many states to provide for the security of individuals and their communities has led to raising insecurity in urban zones. Large-scale urbanization tends to be associated with increased rates of armed violence, and is often coupled with decreasing levels of public safety, posing serious challenges to the provision of security and justice. Increased armed homicides are linked to networks of criminal gangs who are being given access to these weapons. The increase of terrorism has also led to the widespread use of firearms in several incidents that have occurred in the United States.

## Impact

There is a connection between the proliferation of powerful guns and gun-related deaths and injuries. Extra bullets held by high-capacity clips allow the spraying of bullets with the speed of carnage being guaranteed before anyone can intervene. Military assault weapons and high-capacity military-style ammunition clips allow shooters to fire hundreds of rounds in a matter of a minute. Someone who is determined to kill people will find a way to commit mass murders. Even non-fatal shootings, such as serious abdominal gun-shot injuries, require health care that costs many times the normal amount, and which can go on for weeks, months and even years.

## Increasing Lethality

Ammunition is being made more lethal. Rip, dum-dum, hollow-point, bonded, jacketed and polymer-tipped bullets are being made in ever increasing quantities. The firearms themselves are becoming very lethal. These include firearms such as the Kalashnikov AK-47, the Thompson machine gun, the M16 rifle, the F-2000 assault rifle and the Uzi sub-machine gun. Handguns are also becoming more powerful and include weapons such as the Glock, Beretta, Colt, Smith & Wesson, Magnum, Desert Eagle and revolvers.

## Registration of Firearms

Federal gun laws in the United States regulate the sale, possession, and use of firearms and ammunition. State laws vary considerably, and are independent of existing federal firearm laws, although they are sometimes broader or more limited in scope than the federal laws. State level laws vary significantly in their form, content, and level of restriction. Forty-four states have a provision in their state constitutions similar to the Second Amendment, which protects the right to keep and bear arms. The exceptions are California, Iowa, Maryland, Minnesota, New Jersey, and New York. In New York, however, the statutory civil rights laws contain a provision virtually identical to the Second Amendment. Additionally, the Supreme Court held in the case of *McDonald v. Chicago* in 2010 that the protections of the Second Amendment to keep and bear arms for self-defense in one's home apply against state governments and their political subdivisions.

Firearm owners are subject to the firearm laws of the state they are in, and not exclusively their state of residence. Reciprocity between states exists in certain situations, such as with regard to concealed carry permits. These are recognized on a state-by-state basis. Florida issues a license to carry both concealed weapons and firearms, but others license only the concealed carry of firearms. Some states do not recognize out-of-state permits to carry a firearm. Although state firearms laws are usually considerably less restrictive than federal firearms laws, this does not confer any immunity against prosecution for violations of the federal laws. But, state and local police departments are not legally obligated to enforce federal gun laws as was decided by the Supreme Court in the case of *Pritz v. United States* in 1997.

The problem is that there is no national registration of guns available. For the majority of American gun owners there is no system, database, or registry that ties them to any of the firearms. Even the Brady Act that created the background check system requires that the records of each background check be destroyed within 24 hours. The Firearm Owners' Protection Act of 1986 is a United States federal law that revised many provisions of the Gun Control Act of 1968. This act makes it illegal for the national government or any state in the country to keep any sort of database or registry that ties firearms directly to their owner.

The problem is exacerbated by the existence of "ghost guns", weapons that are built form firearm parts. These weapons use a kit gun, with no serial numbers. These weapons are assembled at home, allowing owners to avoid registering them. Gun kits, which involve a weapon that is already 80% completed, with the remaining 20% to be assembled at home, are legal to buy.

Another problem is with respect to plastic guns. Plastic guns are manufactured with 3-D printers. Again, there is no serial number that can trace these weapons to their owners. But, the biggest problem is that these guns are not detectable by scanning devices, thus allowing anyone with a plastic gun to enter into a place that has monitoring equipment for metal guns. The lack of national registration coupled with plastic and ghost guns makes the problem of determining who owns weapons almost impossible, especially when they are used to commit crimes.

# Police Forces

Today police radios have scanners that use 30 different channels and police officers have in-car video cameras, traffic monitoring radar units, in-car computer data terminals with Internet access, body cameras, department-issued cellphones and personal cellphones and tablets. Even so, social media and other applications have also made it possible for gangs and terrorist organizations to coordinate like never before, creating an entirely new digital space that needs policing. Traffic-tracking tools that display the current location of police officers allow those with criminal intent to avoid or seek out and harm law enforcement personnel. Police are being tasked with increasingly complicated challenges as the state of technology evolves.

A new armament of tools in the fight against crime is needed that will radically alter the way that law enforcement operates. This includes 3D crime scene imaging to replace sketches and photographs, through-the-wall radar to detect movement, body-worn cameras to prevent false claims of inappropriate behavior or abuse, and the use of predictive analytics by using software dedicated to providing insight into criminal patterns as well as all legally warranted personal information. Other newer techniques that should be used include crime lights to detect hair, fibers, and body fluids at crime scenes, in-car camera systems to confirm and ensure a high degree of officer professionalism, photo enforcement systems to generate red light violations and/or speeding summons, graffiti cameras that can take photographs of suspects who are vandalizing property, thermal imaging systems to produce images of radiated or reflected surface energy, language translators, specialty impact munitions, chemical agents and projectile systems for chemical agents, GPS tracking devices, and K-9 unit cameras. New developments in police drones, brain fingerprinting, handheld fingerprint scanners, and Google Glass for taking photographs are needed to equip modern police forces.

Of great importance is the design for new body armor, especially with the very lethal weapons and ammunition that police officers have to face these days. Protective vests for law enforcement officers include ballistic-resistant and stab-resistant body armor that provides coverage and protection for the torso. Ballistic-resistant body armor protects against bullet penetrations and the blunt trauma associated with bullet impacts can be added to vests that include soft body armor, which protects against handgun bullets and less flexible tactical armor composed of soft and hard components that protect against rifle bullets. Stab-resistant body armor protects against knives and spikes. The kinds of threats that officers will likely face in the future requires much better body armor with suitable properties to protect against those threats—especially against terrorists with high-powered weapons. SWAT team members might need body armor that offers a much higher level of protection than the body armor worn for regular duty by police officers. Riot gear suits with very tough metal helmets, shin guards and gloves need to be worn by officers who respond to civil disturbances.

All of this requires money to equip the police forces in all fifty states. Again, most cities and states do not have the required cash to maintain the high level of police gear, systems and high-tech systems that are needed by today's law enforcement personnel. The federal government must step in to ensure that a high degree of training, equipment and weaponry is available for the police forces in America.

The fundamental issue with police forces is with respect to the interactions between the police and citizenry—especially with regard to the law. In recent Supreme Court rulings, the issues have centered on restraints on police. In one of these cases, the Supreme Court decided that evidence seized in illegal searches obtained in violation of the Fourth Amendment may not be used in state law criminal prosecutions in state courts, or in federal criminal law prosecutions in federal courts. In another case, the Supreme Court required that certain rights of a person interrogated while in police custody be clearly explained, including the right to an attorney. In still another ruling, the Supreme Court required a search warrant in cases of domestic surveillance. In 1985, the Supreme Court ruled that police could not shoot fleeing criminal suspects who were unarmed and not considered dangerous. With respect to interrogation rights, in 1990 the Supreme Court ruled that once a person has requested a lawyer, then no further police interrogation could take place until the lawyer was present. In 2000, the Supreme Court ruled that an anonymous tip that a person is carrying a gun is not sufficient to justify a police officer's stop and frisk of that person. In 2006, the Supreme Court ruled that if police do not have a warrant, they cannot search a home if one of the occupants' objects, even if another grants police permission. In 2001, the Supreme Court declared as unconstitutional police roadblocks that are set up to catch drug offenders and detect illegal drugs, ruling that they violate privacy rights of innocent motorists.

In other areas the Supreme Court has expanded the police powers. In 1993, the Supreme Court ruled that police may seize nonthreatening contraband that was detected through the sense of touch during a protective pat down search—as long as there was justification that the person may be armed and dangerous. In 1998, the Supreme Court ruled that a police officer does not violate substantive due process by causing death through deliberate or reckless indifference to life in a high-speed automobile chase aimed at apprehending a suspected offender. In 1999, the Supreme Court ruled that police officers with probable cause to search a car may inspect passengers' belongings found in the car that are capable of concealing the object of the search. In 1999, the Supreme Court ruled that the Fourth Amendment does not require the police to obtain a warrant before seizing an automobile from a public place when they have probable cause to believe that it is forfeitable contraband. In 2004, the Supreme Court rejected the argument that the Fourth Amendment's protection against unreasonable search and seizure and the Fifth Amendment's right against self-incrimination do not allow a person suspected of being involved in a crime to refuse to identify himself to the police. In 2006, the Supreme Court ruled that even if police fail to knock and announce before entering a home to execute a search warrant, evidence obtained in the search may be admitted at trial. in 2009, the Supreme Court held that police may conduct a pat down search of a passenger in an automobile that has been lawfully stopped for a minor traffic violation, provided the police suspect that the passenger is armed and dangerous. In 2014, the Supreme Court ruled that the police need warrants to search the cellphones of people that they arrest.

In 2012, the Supreme Court upheld a law, which allows police officers to ask the immigration status of any person suspected of a crime. In 2013, the Supreme Court held that when officers make an arrest supported by probable cause to hold for a serious offense and bring the suspect to the station to be detained in custody, then taking and analyzing a cheek swab of the arrestee's DNA is like fingerprinting and photographing, and is a legitimate police booking procedure under the Fourth Amendment. In 2016, the Supreme Court ruled in favor of police searches without a warrant in cases where a pre-existing warrant for an individual arrest is valid—even if the officer's conduct is considered unconstitutional. In 2018, the Supreme Court ruled that police officers must generally have a warrant before searching vehicles parked at a private home or on its surrounding property.

Recent disturbances in which police have killed unarmed African-Americans have cause much alienation. Better education, such as more sensitivity training, needs to be done at all of the police stations across the land. The hiring of more minorities is essential to decrease the level of confrontation in the streets. The promotion of more minorities is a definite requirement to allay people's fears of being subjected to discrimination and abuse. The interactions between police and citizens are always subject to result in bloodshed if the results are altercations—especially with an increasingly armed populace. Many police officers have been killed by being gunned down while performing their duties. Stricter laws that protect policemen are needed lest we become a "wild west" civilization.

# Malnutrition

## Overview

Despite the relative abundance of food in the United States, there are still some areas that have problems of malnutrition. Malnutrition is a condition that results from eating a diet in which one or more nutrients are either not enough such that the diet causes health problems by lack of calories, protein. carbohydrates, vitamins or minerals. If malnutrition occurs during pregnancy, or in the very early years of living, it may result in permanent problems with physical and mental development. The extreme of malnutrition involves gradual starvation that results in a short height, thin body, poor energy levels, and swollen legs and abdomen. Frequent infections and colds are the symptoms of malnutrition. Undernourishment is most often due to not enough high-quality food being available to eat, which is mostly related to high food prices and poverty.

Efforts to improve nutrition are underway in some areas of the United States The purpose is to get food to people who need it the most, and to provide money or food stamps so that people can buy food within local markets. Simply feeding students by lunch programs at school is insufficient to combat malnutrition since often that are deprived of meals at home due to poverty.

Malnutrition increases the risk of infection and infectious disease, and moderate malnutrition weakens every part of the immune system. In communities or areas that lack safe drinking water, malnutrition presents a critical problem. Lower energy and impaired function of the brain represent the downward spiral of malnutrition as victims are less able to perform the tasks that they need to in order to acquire food, earn an income, or gain an education. Malnutrition can lead to acquiring diseases such as hypoglycemia, which can cause lethargy, limpness, convulsion, or loss of consciousness. Gastroenteritis, parasite infections and diarrhea can result through decreased nutrient absorption. Malnutrition can cause cognitive impairments, anemia and other defects like iodine deficiency and disabling goiters. Maternal malnutrition can also factor into the poor health or death of a baby due to lack of nutritious foods for the mother such as milk, meat, poultry and fruits.

Food banks and soup kitchens address malnutrition in places where people lack money to buy food. A basic income has been proposed as a way to ensure that everyone has enough money to buy food and other basic needs. It is a form of social security in which all citizens or residents regularly receive an unconditional sum of money, either from a government or some other public institution, in addition to any income received from elsewhere.

## Special Populations Affected by Malnutrition

<u>Children</u>

Malnutrition in the first two years is irreversible. Malnourished children grow up with worse health and lower education achievement. Malnutrition also exacerbates the problems of diseases such as measles, pneumonia and diarrhea, and chronic malnutrition can actually be fatal in its own right. As underweight children are more vulnerable to almost all infectious diseases, the indirect disease burden of malnutrition is critical, especially when coupled with unsafe water, bad sanitation and unclean hygiene practices.

Women

Malnutrition in women is associated with poverty, lack of development and awareness, and illiteracy. Gender discrimination in households can also prevent a woman's access to sufficient food and healthcare. Women also have unique nutritional requirements, and in some cases need more nutrients than men; such as calcium.

The Elderly

Malnutrition and being underweight are more common in the elderly. Changes in body composition, organ functions, adequate energy intake and ability to eat or access food are associated with aging, and may contribute to malnutrition. Sadness or depression can play a role, causing changes in appetite, digestion, energy level, weight, and well-being.

Malnutrition in the elderly can result from gastrointestinal and endocrine system disorders, loss of taste and smell, decreased appetite and inadequate dietary intake. Poor dental health, ill-fitting dentures, or chewing and swallowing problems can make eating difficult. As a result of these factors, malnutrition is seen to develop more easily in the elderly.

One of the main requirements of elderly care is to provide an adequate diet and all essential nutrients. Many elderly people require assistance in eating, which may contribute to malnutrition, especially when there is insufficient social care, in which vulnerable people are at home or in care homes that are not helped to eat.

Malnutrition and weight loss can contribute to sarcopenia, with loss of lean body mass and muscle function. Abdominal obesity or weight loss coupled with sarcopenia can lead to immobility, skeletal disorders, insulin resistance, hypertension, atherosclerosis, and metabolic disorders.

# Poverty

Poverty is not having enough material possessions or income for a person's needs, an is related to social, economic, and political elements. Absolute poverty is the complete lack of the means necessary to meet basic personal needs, such as food, clothing and shelter. Relative poverty occurs when a person cannot meet a minimum level of living standards. The United States government has tried to reduce poverty, most notably by the Great Society program of the 1960s. However, providing basic needs to people who are unable to earn a sufficient income can be hampered by constraints on the government's ability to deliver services, such as corruption, tax avoidance, debt and loan defaults. Strategies of increasing income to make basic needs more affordable typically include welfare and other social programs of government assistance.

Although the United States is a wealthy country, poverty has consistently been present throughout, along with efforts to alleviate it, from New Deal-era legislation to the War on Poverty in the 1960s, and to poverty alleviation efforts during the 2008 Great Recession, which increased poverty levels. New and extreme forms of poverty have emerged in the United States as a result of structural adjustment policies and globalization, which have rendered economically marginalized communities into destitute surplus populations.

The United States' high poverty rate needs to be tackled by raising the minimum wage. As many as 30% of Americans have trouble making ends meet and 38% of Americans live "paycheck to paycheck". 60% of working-class Americans lived below the intermediate budget, which allows for replacement of transportation, home appliances, home repairs and other replacement costs. 40% of Americans do not have $400 available for an emergency as their budgets allow nothing for savings. This is a very dire situation, especially if medical care is necessitated. Added to this are the high costs of living and the very high home prices and rents that are making more people homeless. Even on Native American reservations, poverty is very high. Poverty among the elderly is also rising because social security benefits are insufficient to meet the rising costs of everything. Also, many teenagers in low income communities are often forced to join gangs, save school lunches, sell drugs or exchange sexual favors because they cannot afford food.

But, the worst part concerns child poverty, especially when 3½ million children under the age of 5 are at risk of hunger in the United States, and more than 20% in 11 states are at the risk of going hungry, especially in households headed by single mothers. 31 million low-income children receive free or reduced-price meals daily through the National School lunch program, and 14 million children are served by Feeding America program. Also, 2½ million children have experienced homelessness The effects of poverty are many, including access to quality education, higher incarceration rates, lowering of IQ, dilapidated housing, no employment opportunities, and development of diseases such as hookworm. All of this behooves the government to undertake efforts to reduce poverty and its effects, especially since the United States has the weakest social safety net of all the developed nations.

# Population Ageing

Population ageing is a shift in the distribution of population towards older ages. It represents an increasing median age in a population in which the aged population is at its highest level in American history. The number of people aged 60 years and over has tripled since 1950. It not known whether the older population is living the extra years of life in good or in poor health. In any case, the nation is now aware of the ageing of its population and the implications which this will have on their lives and the lives of their children and grandchildren.

The number of Americans ages 65 and older will more than double over the next 40 years, reaching 80 million in 2040. The number of adults ages 85 and older, the group most often needing help with basic personal care, will quadruple between 2000 and 2040. More older adults will exist than kids by 2035. With this swelling number of older adults, the country will see greater demands for healthcare, in-home caregiving and assisted living facilities. It will also affect Social Security, with a projection of 3½ working-age adults for every older person eligible for Social Security in 2020. It also means increased health care costs.

This requires digital innovations to tackle some of the problems, such as remote patient monitoring devices that include voice apps to remind diabetes patients to take their insulin. These same apps allow doctors to monitor their conditions. Some seniors also wear digital blood pressure cuffs that remotely send their blood pressure and pulse to doctors with no action required on the patient's part other than to simply wear the cuff.

Cutting-edge technology is also infiltrating home care, specifically assisted living facilities. Voice assistants such as the Amazon Echo/Alexa and Google Home help senior citizens remember their daily schedules, such as when to eat, take their medication, or go to their doctors' appointments. Smart pillboxes help with dosage amounts and timing. Smart clothing can help doctors monitor their patients' movements to check for irregular walking, or to send an alert if the person falls. Beyond that, motion detectors, smart mattresses, and even personal robots can help make the assisted living experience more pleasant in the seniors' later years. Digital health is at the forefront of transformation in the healthcare industry, both as a driver of and an answer to the challenges industry players are grappling with. All of the industry's major players, including payers, providers, and manufacturers, are affected by healthcare's digital transformation.

A confluence of forces will induce healthcare's embrace of digital health, and will lower healthcare costs. Tech-focused entrants into healthcare will act as catalysts for change. Key digital health solutions like EHRs, digital therapeutics, telehealth, AI, wearables, and block chain are the foundation of the industry's digital transformation. Digital health should be able to address many of the challenges that are going to be experienced by an aging population.

# Immigration

Overview

Immigration in the United States is on the rise, even as new roadblocks are imposed to lower the number of entrants into the country. Migration is beneficial and has positive economic effects if handled correctly. In the United States immigration either has no impact on the crime rate and may even reduce it. There is a considerable amount of assimilation for both first- and second-generation immigrants. But, there is discrimination against foreign born and minority populations in criminal justice, business, the economy, housing, health care, and the media in the United States. The politics of immigration have become increasingly associated with other issues, such as national security and terrorism. The treatment of migrants in the United States by federal agencies, by employers, and by the original population is a topic of much debate, and contains many instances of violation of migrant human rights as the crisis deepens.

Main Issues

Some proponents of immigration argue that the freedom of movement is a basic human right, and that the restrictive immigration policies violate this human right of freedom of movement. Immigration policies which selectively grant freedom of movement to targeted individuals are intended to produce a net economic gain. The support behind the notion that low-skilled immigration, while creating winners and losers, makes the average American better off. Is that Immigrants often do types of work that native populations are unwilling to do. In this manner, immigrants contribute to greater economic prosperity for the economy as a whole: Immigrants are also more likely to work in risky jobs than native workers.

Competition from immigrants in a particular profession may aggravate underemployment in that profession, But, diversity and immigration have a net positive effect on productivity. Nevertheless, low-skill immigration has been linked to greater income inequality, and immigrant refugees tend to do worse in economic terms than natives, even when they have the same skills and language proficiencies of natives. The economic effects of undocumented immigrants are generally positive for the native population and public coffers. Increasing deportation rates and tightening border control weakens low-skilled labor markets, increasing the unemployment of native low-skilled workers. Legalization of undocumented workers decreases the unemployment rate of low-skilled natives and increases income per native. Undocumented immigrants to the United States generate a higher surplus for American firms relative to natives, so restricting their entry has a depressing effect on job creation, and in turn, on native labor markets.

Of the estimated 15 million undocumented immigrants in the United States, 11 million are included in the Deferred Action for Parents of Americans (DAPA) category. The government policy to enable them to stay was prevented from going into effect. 800,000 more are included in the Deferred Action for Childhood Arrivals (DACA) category, which has also been blocked as to eligibility for staying in the country.

# Racism

## Overview

Racism is the belief that groups of humans possess different behavioral traits corresponding to physical appearance, and which can be divided based on the superiority of one group over another. It entails discrimination, prejudice and antagonism directed against other people because they are different. Racism is often based on learned social perceptions of biological differences between peoples. The effects manifest themselves in the form of social actions, practices, beliefs, marking of ethnicities, or cultural, institutional, economic and political systems in which differences are ranked as inherently superior or inferior to each other based on presumed shared inheritable traits, abilities, or qualities. In its worst form, it involves violence perpetrated against those who are different.

## A Brief History of Racism in the United States

Racism in the United States has existed since the colonial era. The slavery of African-Americans, the destruction of Indian cultures, barriers that were placed against immigrants, the internment of Asians and Hispanics, and the hostility against Arabs as a result of terrorist actions have all been based on racism. The primary groups that have been affected by racism are as follows:

### African-Americans

From the time of the Pilgrims blacks have been enslaved. The South came to rely on black slave labor for their economic ventures, especially farming and crop production. In 1865, 4 million blacks were emancipated, but the racism persisted, especially in the South. Blacks were blamed for the Civil War, and black codes, Jim Crow laws, paramilitary groups, organizations like the KKK, and segregation with separate facilities all served to deprive blacks of their freedom and rights—in spite of federal legislation like Civil Rights Acts and Constitutional Amendments. Even after the Supreme Court ruling in 1954 in the case of *Brown v Board of Education* did little to overcome these entrenched racial divisions. It wasn't until the rise of the Civil Rights Movement that things began to change. But, even the election of Barack Obama has not altered the supremacy advocates who have been emboldened by the election of Donald Trump and his policies.

### Native Americans

From the time that the first European settlers arrived in America, Native Americans have been subjected to removal and annihilation. After the creation of the United States, the idea of removing the Indians to the West side of the Mississippi gained momentum. Through Indian wars, displacements, broken treaties and destruction of their habitations, thousands of Native Americans were subjected to maltreatment, which many times resulted in death. Those who were left behind suffered the marginalization of being confined to reservations, being stripped of their heritage, and being forced to assimilate into the dominant culture. The Indians were not even considered as citizens until 1924 when the Indian Citizenship Act was passed by Congress. But, even with formal recognition, Indians remain among the most economically disadvantaged groups in the country—and they are subjected to discrimination, especially in the courts.

Asians

The Chinese people have been discriminated against in many ways. **The Naturalization Act of 1790 was passed by Congress that made Asians ineligible for citizenship.** Yet, thousands were brought into the country in the 1800s as "coolies" to work on various projects, mines, and railways. When too many Chinese workers were brought into the country, Congress passed the Chinese Exclusion Act in 1882 to ban the immigration of Chinese laborers.

Japanese immigrants began in 1907 to enter the United States in large numbers, filling jobs that were once filled by Chinese workers. This influx led to discrimination, causing President Theodore Roosevelt to restrict Japanese immigration. Later, Japanese immigration was closed when the United States stopped issuing passports to Japanese workers who were intending to move to the United States. During WWII after the Pearl Harbor attack by the Japanese military, thousands of Japanese were rounded up, primarily on the West Coast of the United States, and were placed into internment camps because of possible security threats—even though the vast majority of them were United States citizens who were loyal to the country.

Prejudice and Asian racism affected United States policy in the Korean and Vietnam Wars, even though Asians were on both sides of those conflicts as well as in WWII. A climate of racism ensued that allowed for a pattern in which Asian civilians were treated as less than human, with war crimes becoming common.

Europeans

Various European immigrant groups have been subjected to discrimination either on the basis of their immigrant status, or on the basis of their ethnicity. In the 19th century, anti-Irish prejudice was rampant. During the 1830s in the United States, riots over control of job sites broke between Irish and local American work teams who were competing for construction jobs. During both WWI and WWII, German-Americans were barred from many activities because of being accused of having political allegiances to Germany. The Polish were also discriminated against because of their ethnicity.

Hispanics

After the Mexican–American War that took place between 1846 and 1848, the United States annexed much of the Southwestern region from Mexico. Mexicans residing in that territory then found themselves subject to discrimination—even though some of them had resided in these areas for almost 300 years. During WWII, Mexican laborers were brought into the United States to alleviate the labor shortage in agriculture. But, after the war ended, the United States policy shifted towards returning them to Mexico. Even in the 20th century, many public institutions, businesses, and home owners' associations had official policies to exclude Mexican-Americans. School children of Mexican-American descent were subjected to racial segregation in the public school system. In many areas across the Southwest, they lived in separate residential areas, due to laws and real estate company policies that excluded them from prime locations, leading to the rise of barrios.

Jewish-Americans

Antisemitism has played a major role in the United States. During the late 19th and early 20th centuries, hundreds of thousands of ethnic Jews escaped the pogroms in Europe. They boarded boats and arrived at Ellis Island, New York where they were subjected to racism by the port immigration authorities. Beginning in the 1910s, Southern Jewish communities were attacked by the KKK, which objected to Jewish immigration. During WWII, many more Jews escaped from Germany as the Nazi regime became bent on eliminating them. In recent times, a new antisemitism has evolved from neo-Nazi groups, which has sometimes resulted in violence against Jewish people, with some of them being killed by members of these groups.

Arab-Americans

Following the 9-11 attacks in the United States, discrimination and racialized violence has markedly increased against Arab Americans. Muslims have been demonized to the point that much hatred towards Middle Easterners living in the United States has ensued. Racial profiling has become a growing problem for Arab-Americans, particularly in airports where they are often subjected to heightened security screening, pre-boarding searches and interrogations, and who are sometimes denied passage based solely on the belief that ethnicity or national origin increases passengers' flight risk.

Iranian-Americans

After the 1979 Iranian hostage crisis of the United States embassy in Tehran, Iran took place, it precipitated a wave of anti-Iranian sentiment in the United States, directed both against Iranian nationals and immigrants. Even though such sentiments declined after the release of the hostages in 1981, they have sometimes flared up with situations that vilify Iranians—especially by the media and the movie industry. Current tensions with the Middle East conflicts that are ongoing have only served to intensify the feelings of hostility towards those Iranians.

Indian-Americans

Stereotyping and scapegoating of Indian Americans have been conducted in recent years. In particular, racial discrimination against Indian-Americans in the workplace has occurred due to the rise in outsourcing and offshoring activities whereby Indian-Americans are blamed for United States companies hiring workers from India. Many

Indian-Americans have been subjected to a backlash of implicit racial discrimination, and numerous cases of religious stereotyping of American Hindus have occurred.

## The Consequences of Racism

Racism is detrimental to everyone. Popular culture has created and perpetuated negative stereotypes of minorities. Immigration quotas have been substantially reduced recently, and a push toward deportation of undocumented persons—who are mostly minorities—has taken prime importance. Even a massive border fence is being erected on the border between Mexico and the United States to presumably stop the flow of illegals from Mexico, Guatemala, El Salvador, Nicaragua and other Latin-American countries. There are also major racial differences in access to health care and in the quality of health care that is provided. Racial disparities have been noted in all levels of the United States justice system. Hate crimes have increased by the specific targeting of minorities because of their identity.

There is an abundance of societal and political suggestions to alleviate the effects of continued racial discrimination in the United States—none of which has worked. There is no foreseeable solution to this problem. All that can be said is that *we must view each other as spiritual beings—for that is who we really are*.

# Crime

A crime, which is defined as an unlawful act that is punishable by a state or other authority, is an offense that is harmful not only to some individual but also to a community, society, or the state. Acts such as murder, rape, and theft are to be prohibited for the protection of society. The state has the power to restrict one's liberty for committing a crime, and if found guilty, an offender may be sentenced to reparation, imprisonment, or even execution. When informal relationships prove insufficient to establish and maintain a desired social order, a state may impose stricter systems of social control that can compel populations to conform to codes, and it can opt to punish or attempt to reform those who do not conform.

The huge problem is the prevention of crime through legal remedies and sanctions under a criminal justice system. Since a crime is an act that the population perceives based on societal norms, the deviant behavior that violates these norms must be dealt with the penal responses that are made by society as a preemptive harm-reduction action by using the threat of punishment as a deterrent to anyone proposing to engage in a criminal behavior that causes harm. In theory, this appears fine, but there are several obstacles in fighting crime:

- Even if victims recognize their own role as victims, they may not have the resources to investigate and seek legal redress for the injuries that they suffered.

- The victims may only want compensation for the injuries suffered, while remaining indifferent to a possible desire for deterrence.

- The fear of retaliation by the perpetrators may deter victims or witnesses of crimes from taking any action.

- If offenders have sufficient wealth, they can circumvent the enforcement of laws by hiring criminal lawyers.

- As a result of the crime, victims may die or become incapacitated, and may be unable to respond.

- A crime may be perpetrated from emotional or psychological reasons.

With the proliferation of weapons in the United States, it is becoming more difficult to prevent crimes. Also, gun laws that allow the indiscriminate purchase of weapons and the concealment of these weapons allow perpetrators to pick their targets at random. If the economy takes a downturn, then what will follow are more robberies, burglaries, holdups, and property thefts. The prevention of crime is a very serious and difficult problem, with no conceivable solution in sight—other than to build more jails and lock people up.

**Environmental Concerns**

# Dealing with the Environment

## Water Resources

Two big factors in helping the environment are desalination plants and pollution controls. Saltwater can be desalinated to produce drinking water as well as water to irrigate crops. Currently, due to its energy consumption, desalinating seawater is more costly than fresh water that is obtained from rivers or groundwater, water recycling and water conservation. But, the depletion of water reserves is a critical problem as scarcity of water resources increases. Distillation and reverse osmosis are two methods that are used, but they are costly in terms of energy prices for infrastructure and maintenance that must be paid to accomplish the process. Also, desalination removes iodine from water, which could lead to iodine deficiency disorders. Further research needs to be done to improve the process, such as by using waste heat, ocean thermal energy, solar power and greenhouse condensation methodologies. Other approaches that might prove promising involve using geothermal, nanotube membranes, biomimetic processes, electrochemical, freezing and electro kinetic waves.

## Pollution Control

Pollution control has many forms such as abatement of noise, removal of chemical substances, reduction of gases produced by gas, oil and coal, littering control, disposal of radioactive materials, lowering of thermal outputs, and elimination of over-illuminated regions. The cost of pollution is enormous, especially with air pollution that is caused by automobile and industrial emissions. Soil and water contaminants are also harmful, especially from toxic materials that seep into groundwater.

The main issue with pollution control is the cost that is associated in the implementation of pollution control devices. There are many methods of achieving pollution control that can be done with existing technologies. Automobile emissions can be curtailed to a minimum with relatively inexpensive catalytic converters, better engine designs, and less toxic gasoline fuels. Electric cars offer the best solution to gas emissions, and will be made even more efficient with the introduction of more powerful and less expensive batteries. Airplanes can be made more fuel efficient while at the same time producing less of a carbon footprint in the atmosphere. It is a matter of placing human health as a priority.

# Destruction of the Oceans

## Overview

The oceans are in a crisis by having been exploited through overfishing. Warming ocean temperature levels have also killed one-fourth of all the world's coral reefs, and in the process an enormous amount of sea life has been made extinct. The large-scale exploitation of the oceans by commercial fishing has eliminated 90% of the world's large fish, including tuna and marlin, as well as species such as cod and halibut. The decimation of tuna is particularly important since they eat jellyfish. With a lack of substantial numbers of tuna, the jellyfish have proliferated to the point where they are a threat to the world's coastal ecosystems.

## Elimination of Species

Some of the most valuable and prized large fish species such as swordfish have been all but been eliminated everywhere in the world. If present fishing levels persist, and harmful fishing practices are continued, then the oceans will be deprived of invaluable marine life and habitats. The harmful fishing practices include the discard of several million tons of fish every year in the process of commercial fishing, and the use of bottom trawling fishing gear, which is causing indiscriminate and systematic destruction of ocean habitats around the world. Contributing to the decimation is the vanishing of 90% of the wetlands, which are the nurseries for fish. Toxic substances such as PCBs are causing tumors in sea life, some sea mammals are being infected by parasites, and other sea mammals are becoming sick by eating toxic algae.

## Pollution Effects

The oceans are being threatened by marine pollution. The uncontrolled dumping of trash is creating several dead zones in the oceans where no life can exist. Toxic spills and oil spills have produced devastating effects by affecting the food chain, and by creating dead zones where oxygen has been deprived. Once the food web is destroyed in the ocean, there is no repair process, and the harmful effects will spread beyond the immediate affected area.

The worst form of pollution is called mermaid tears, which are small pieces of glass or plastic found in the world's oceans. When bottles, cups, or other debris are dumped into the water, they often break apart—but they don't decompose into biodegradable material. Instead, the pieces are worn down by the tumbling of the waves and sand, and eventually they form into smooth, rounded shapes. As they get smaller and smaller, mermaid tears become more harmful to more organisms in the sea as these tiny chunks of plastic are widely distributed in the oceans. Some of the plastic debris may contain chemical pollutants.

The most harmful results occur when these particles are ingested by marine animals who cannot digest them. As a result, smaller organisms can die with large numbers of mermaid tears in their digestive tracts. Bigger organisms may consume this plastic when they eat these smaller organisms, and the plastic then becomes widely distributed as it is passed up into the marine food chain—and into the human food chain. Every year, 8 million tons of plastic are being deposited into the oceans by being blown from garbage dumps into rivers and estuaries, and then carried to the oceans, or by being discarded on beaches and along coastlines. With more than 64 million tons of trash reaching the oceans every year, this problem becomes greater, especially since plastics last forever because they do not biodegrade.

## The Impacts

The world's oceans are under a threat from global warming, declining oxygen levels and acidification. The oceans have continued to warm, pushing many commercial fish stocks towards the poles and raising the risk of extinction for some marine species. The scale and rate of the present day carbon deviation, and resulting ocean acidification, is unprecedented in Earth's history. The oceans are warming because of heat from a build-up of greenhouse gases in the atmosphere. Fertilizers and sewage that wash into the oceans are causing blooms of algae to thrive that reduce oxygen levels in the waters. Also, $CO_2$ in the air forms a weak acid when it reacts with seawater.

Acidification threatens marine organisms that use calcium carbonate to build their skeletons, such as reef-forming corals, crabs, oysters and some plankton that are vital to marine food webs. Corals may cease to grow if worldwide temperatures rise by just 2 degrees Celsius and would start to dissolve at 3 degrees Celsius. Temperatures have already risen by one degree Celsius.

Oceans contain more than 97% of the planet's water and produce more than one-half of the oxygen that we breathe. Oceans absorb carbon, which is important in reducing global warming. One-half of the world's people live in coastal zones, and ocean-based businesses contribute more than $500 billion every year to the global economy. As ocean levels rise due to the melting of large glaciers, these coastal zones will be impacted by rising sea levels.

## Plastic Debris

Plastic debris is accumulating in the oceans in great quantities. Items such as hard hats, fishing nets, tires, tooth brushes and plastic bottle containers have created at least 5 huge garbage patches that are drifting in some areas of the ocean. Most of these garbage patches are made up of tiny fragments of plastic. 80% of the debris comes from land-based activities. Sea creatures get trapped in the larger pieces of debris in these garbage patches and die.

Plastic accumulates on the sea floor and in sediments, washes up on coastlines and is taken up by fish and other sea life. Plastic affects birds, fish, mammals and other marine life. It eventually breaks down into smaller bits, and can look like fish eggs such that they get eaten by marine animals, which is problematic because plastic releases estrogenic compounds to everything it comes in contact with. Hundreds of species mistake plastics for their natural food, and ingest toxicants that cause liver and stomach abnormalities in fish and birds, often choking them to death.

## Overfishing

Human beings are sea creatures, dependent on the oceans just as much as whales, herring or coral reefs. The oceans represent 97% of the biosphere where life exists, providing the water we use and the air that we breathe. But, destructive fishing techniques are threatening the biodiversity of the oceans. Tuna takes 10 to 14 years to mature, requires thousands of pounds of food to develop. But, they are being hunted to the point of extinction. Krill, a vital food sources for sea life, is also being harvested in vast quantities, with trawlers traveling halfway around the globe and generating carbon emissions.

## Trawling

Bottom trawling is a process that brings untold damage to sea beds that support ocean life. Trawling is destroying a whole ecosystem and turning coral reefs into rubble, which is killing sponges. Bottom trawls and dredges are so destructive because they effectively clear-cut everything that is living on the seafloor. Trawls and dredges use large, heavy nets kept open by doors, weighing as much as several tons each, many of which drag across large areas of seafloor to catch fish that live on or near the ocean floor. Fishermen use trawls to catch species such as shrimp, cod, haddock, flounder, pollock and rockfish. Dredges are also used to catch scallops, clams, urchins and other species.

Trawling is a particularly destructive fishing technique in terms of discards, bycatch, and collapse of fish stocks, causing serious damage to delicate marine ecosystems. The trawling fleet is estimated to represent more than 15,000 vessels. In terms of destructive trawling, the destructive impact exceeds the protein that is acquired by this technique.

## Deep Sea Mining

Deep-sea mining is adding to the disaster. Deep-sea mining in sea beds causes damage to deep sea ecosystems and creates pollution by heavy metal sediment plumes. Plumes are caused when the tailings from mining are dumped back into the ocean, creating a cloud of particles floating in the water. Near bottom plumes occur when the tailings are pumped back down to the mining site. The floating particles increase the cloudiness of the water, clogging filter-feeding apparatuses used by benthic organisms. Surface plumes cause a more serious problem. Depending on the size of the particles and water currents the surface plumes spread over vast areas. These surface plumes impact zooplankton and decrease the amount of light penetration into the oceans, which in turn affects the food web of the area. The removal of parts of the sea floor results in increasing the toxicity of the water and creating sediment plumes from tailings. Removing parts of the sea floor disturbs the habitat of benthic organisms. There are also leakages, spills and corrosion, which affect the sea organisms in the area.

## Acidification of the Oceans

A huge factor of increasing concern for global change is the acidification of the oceans as they take up carbon dioxide from the atmosphere. There is 50 times more carbon in the oceans than previously existed. The carbon constantly exchanges between the oceans and the atmosphere, causing more acidification. A more acidic ocean will harm marine biodiversity and will accelerate global warming. As the steeply rising curve of carbon dioxide in the atmosphere continues unchecked, the warming of our planet will continue to occur.

# Global Warming

## Climate Effect

Mankind is responsible for 95% of global warming. The accumulation of greenhouse gases—especially $CO_2$—over the past century, mostly by the burning of fossil fuels, has produced a continuously increasing warming effect in the air and on the waters of the planet. In turn, this has produced secondary effects such as storm intensification, damage to crops, glacier shrinkage, coral reef destruction, severe droughts, increased flooding, greater damages from intensified wildfires, a resurgence of old diseases, respiratory stress and the creation of new emerging infectious diseases. Although there is uncertainty as to the future possibilities, the dire predictions are that they may include the formation of extreme weather patterns, dramatic climate shifts, and the disruption of the earth's gulf stream cooling mechanism by the melting of the Arctic ice caps. Associated with these effects are a rise in sea levels that will cover coastal lands by the melting of the Antarctic and Greenland areas, renewed ozone depletion, and mass plant and sea mammal extinctions. The resulting economic disruptions will most likely be accompanied by famines and political conflicts that might produce wide-scale events of genocide.

## Observed Changes

Global warming is the observed rise in the average temperature of the Earth's climate system. Much of the evidence shows that the climate system is warming, and that most of this additional energy has gone into ocean warming. The remainder of this increase in energy has melted ice and warmed the continents and atmosphere. Based on current rates of melting, Arctic summers could be ice-free as early as 2025. Climate change will also affect certain ecosystems, including tundra, mangroves and coral reefs.

Global warming is being caused mostly by increasing concentrations of greenhouse gases and other human activities. The effects include a warming global temperature, rising sea levels, increased humidity, changing precipitation levels, increased heat content of the oceans, earlier timing of spring events such as the flowering of plants and expansion of deserts. Warming is expected to be greater over land than over the oceans and will be the greatest in the Arctic. There will also be the continuing retreat of glaciers, permafrost and sea ice as well as the widespread melting of snow and land ice. Other changes include more frequent and extreme weather events including heat waves, droughts, heavy rainfall with floods and heavy snowfalls. Still other changes include ocean acidification and species extinctions due to shifting temperature regimes.

## Impact on Humans

The effects of climate change, which are mostly due to warming or shifts in precipitation patterns, or both, have been detected worldwide. Effects significant to humans include the threat to food security from decreasing crop yields and the abandonment of populated areas due to rising sea levels. Production of wheat and maize globally has already been impacted by climate change. Economic losses due to extreme weather events have increased globally, with crop production being negatively affected in low latitude countries. Other impacts include injuries and loss of life as storms intensify due to global warming. Continued permafrost degradation will likely result in unstable infrastructure in Arctic regions, impacting roads, pipelines and buildings.

Climate change will result in the extinction of many species and reduced diversity of ecosystems. Ocean acidification will threaten coral reefs, fisheries, protected species and other natural resources of value. Long-term effects from ice melting and deglaciation could result in landmasses being no longer depressed by the weight of ice. This could lead to landslides as well as seismic and volcanic events. Even tsunamis could be generated by submarine landslides caused by warmer ocean water. Overall, impact damages to human beings could result in a loss of $50 trillion in the next few years if global warming continues unabated.

The hottest years in recorded history have all occurred recently. If the Arctic and Antarctic ice packs disappear completely, the resultant rise in sea levels will flood much of the world's low-lying coastal areas. The greenhouse effect will make our summers hotter and drier, and our winters colder and wetter. The increase in temperature differentials will swell the atmospheric pressure, which in turn will lead to more winds. The result will be enormous disruptions in weather patterns such as severe droughts, increases in the number and power of hurricanes, cyclones and tornados, and snowstorms and ice storms that will wreak havoc.

# Pollution

## Overview

A great danger for earth and humans is that of pollution. With the devastation of the rain forests, the increased burning of fossil fuels and the addition of pollutants into the atmosphere, we are producing changes in weather patterns, which ultimately could affect the earth dramatically through a series of great climatic alterations. The use of toxic substances and other hazardous chemicals as well as the increased reliance on nuclear fission processes with their lethal radiation byproducts could result in widespread crop damages, water and land pollution, harmful genetic mutations and an increase in sickness and deaths due to these health-altering materials. Even the normal utilization of our everyday needs such as sewage treatment, power sources, gases, liquids, metals and everyday household items like plastics, glass, food additives, preservation agents, cleaning detergents and soaps, plus the ensuing garbage that results from all of this is gradually adding to the increased mass of materials that must be either recycled or safely disposed of.

The industrial revolution gave birth to environmental pollution. Pollution issues escalated as population growth far exceeded the ability of neighborhoods to handle their waste problem. The emergence of factories and consumption of immense quantities of coal gave rise to air pollution and the large volume of industrial chemical discharges added to the growing load of untreated human waste. Automobile-caused smog became a major issue with the burning of oil and gasoline.

Severe incidents of pollution have occurred such as PCB dumping, dioxin contamination, radioactive contamination, oil tanker spills, huge concentrations of plastics in the oceans and chemical sludge effluents. Other major sources of pollution are noise pollution, soil contamination, thermal pollution, water pollution and mercury, which can cause developmental deficits in children and neurologic symptoms in adults. Air pollution is now the cause of over 5,000 deaths in the world *per day*.

Carbon emissions now stand at one-third greater than in the pre-industrial era. This has resulted in global warming, a condition that can potentially produce hotter years, that cumulatively can create the reduction of the polar ice caps and mountain glaciers, and which has the potential to create rising sea levels that can inundate coastal cities and island nations. Air pollution and its associated greenhouse effect can also affect weather patterns by producing more droughts, severe destructive storms and devastating floods.

## Health Consequences

Pollution has had serious consequences such as increasing wildlife mortality, the spread of invasive species and the human ingestion of toxic chemicals. Ozone pollution can cause respiratory disease, cardiovascular disease, throat inflammation, chest pain, and congestion. Water pollution causes deaths, mostly due to contamination of drinking water by untreated sewage. Over one billion people on earth have no access to toilets. Over one billion people lack access to safe drinking water. Pollution causes one million deaths per year around the world. Older people are more prone to getting diseases due to being exposed to air pollution. In particular, those with heart or lung disorders are at additional risk. Children and infants are also at serious risk as lead and other heavy metals can cause neurological problems. Chemical and radioactive substances can cause cancer as well as birth defects. Oil spills can cause skin irritations and rashes. Noise pollution induces hearing loss, high blood pressure, stress and sleep disturbances.

# Atmospheric Changes

## The Evidence

Evidence of climate change is all around us, from the melting polar ice caps to shifts of numerous plants and animals. The world is being altered at an alarming pace, and the key factor that is believed to underlie climate change is increased temperature resulting from increased levels of greenhouse gases in the atmosphere—the "greenhouse effect." The greenhouse effect is due to increased levels of greenhouse gases that intensify an effect, which results in increased global temperature.

Human activities are considerably increasing the levels of atmospheric contaminants. Burning of fossil fuels, such as coal, gasoline, and oil, produces both primary pollutants, which are those directly produced from fossil fuel combustion such as nitrogen dioxide, carbon monoxide and carbon dioxide. Secondary pollutants, which are compounds produced from fossil fuel combustion that undergo secondary chemical reactions, form other pollutants such as ozone and chlorofluorocarbons. Methane is produced by the imperfect combustion of wood products. These primary and secondary atmospheric pollutants are the compounds that contribute to global climate change.

## Impacts

Approximately one-third of the produced carbon dioxide dissolves in the oceans, causing seawater to become more acidic. Ocean acidification creates dead zones that make it more difficult for marine organisms to breathe, and consequently makes it harder for them to find food and to avoid predators. The most severe effects are in oxygen minimum zones at depths of 1000 to 3,000 feet, where oxygen is already present at very low concentrations and where only specialized marine life can thrive.

As greenhouse gases alter plant developmental, insects that colonize those plants may also be affected behaviorally and physiologically. Insects that colonize plants, which are growing under increased carbon dioxide and ozone levels, show dispersals at a lower rate than those living at previous carbon dioxide and ozone levels.

Birds may be imperiled by global climate change, as distributions are altered by increasing temperatures. Bird populations may be influenced in a much more direct manner such as through altered food availability. Increased carbon dioxide levels may alter bird populations through altering their food sources.

In terms of human health, the increasing atmospheric concentrations of carbon dioxide due to the increased combustion of fossil fuels will affect all of humanity. The global warming may result in increases in air pollutants, acid deposition, and exposure to ultraviolet radiation. In turn, these will produce an increase in diseases such as skin cancers and lung disorders.

# Damaging Chemical Effects

## Overview

There are thousands of chemicals today that never existed before in the environment. These manmade—and oftentimes lethal—new compounds affect us in ways that are unknown over long periods of time. These chemicals make their way into the water and land, and even rise to the ozone layer in some cases as a result of gases that are emitted as byproducts. Some of these chemicals react with the ozone layer and cause a decrease to occur in the natural shielding of the earth from the harmful rays of the sun. This decrease in the ozone layer due to chemical effects will inevitably lead to more skin disease, an increase in the rate of blindness, and other sun-related disorders caused by a lack of a protective ozone shield.

## The Exposure

The chemical risks are due to the way that we live, produce and consume, including an increasing dependence on chemical fertilizers and pesticides. Many of these toxic substances accumulate in our bodies as they are passed along by other organisms in the food chain—such as through the eating of fish. These contaminants contribute to birth defects, affect the central nervous system and liver, damage the immune systems and increase the risk of cancer, and possibly even lead to genetic mutations among plants, animals and humans. One of the worst types of chemical pollution is that caused by persistent pollutants such as pesticides and industrial chemicals. Changes in the balance of sex hormones and the induction of cancers are both associated with persistent pollutants such as ammoniac nitrogen, carbon dioxide, cadmium, dioxin, mercury, nitrates, phosphorous, asbestos, lead and PCBs.

## Threat to the Ecosystem

The threat to the ecosystem occurs when contaminated substances are absorbed into the soil and into the ground water system as a result of acid rain. Acid rain, which is created by the use of coal and oil for the production of electricity and automobile transportation, contains many impurities. The effects of acid rain are the lowering of the natural pH levels of lakes and surrounding waterways, which increases the acidity of the water. In turn, this affects fish reproduction, aquatic life and microorganisms. Acid rain washes metals from the soil into the lakes, which then poses even more harmful threats to wildlife and fish. Some of these chemicals seriously affect the quality of the habitats, and some may poison marine life and land animals that thrive on marine life when the concentrations of these toxins are high enough. As these toxins are passed up the food chain, the result is damaged DNA and other malfunctions in human hereditary traits.

# Biological Threats

## Overview

Human actions have affected the environment through which the spread of new diseases have created serious threats to public health. These threats are emanating from pandemics such as HIV, SARS, MERS and the Wuhan coronavirus as well as from epidemics such as tuberculosis, cholera and malaria. Other devastating viral diseases include Ebola, dengue fever, Hantavirus, Lyme disease and the West Nile virus, which are spreading throughout the world. Mutations caused by alterations in animal feeding methodologies have produced new strains of salmonella as well as mad cow disease. The lack of basic sanitation and clean drinking water, the continued sex trade, which spreads diseases, plus wars that destroy the infrastructure of regions all contribute to the deterioration of the biological environment.

## Epidemics

An epidemic is the rapid spread of infectious disease to a large number of people in a given population within a short period of time. Epidemics of infectious disease are generally caused by several factors including a change in the ecology of the host population, or by a genetic change in of an emerging pathogen to a host population.

An epidemic may be restricted to one location. However, if it spreads to other countries or continents and affects a substantial number of people, it then becomes a pandemic. Some types of epidemics are diseases such as influenza. However, an epidemic disease may not be contagious such as West Nile fever, which is transmitted by mosquitoes.

The conditions which govern the outbreak of epidemics include infected food supplies such as contaminated drinking water and the migration of populations of certain animals, such as rats or mosquitoes, which can act as disease spreaders. Certain epidemics occur at certain seasons such as whooping-cough, which occurs in spring, and measles, which produces an epidemic in winter and spring. Influenza, the common cold, and other infections of the upper respiratory tract, such as sore throat, occur predominantly in winter.

The most common form of transmission for an epidemic is via an airborne method, with the spread of infection being done through droplets or dust in the air. Another common method of transmission is through insects and rodents. A third method of transmission is by contact by drinking contaminated water or by inhalation while traveling in enclosed spaces such as trains, buses, airplanes and ships. A fourth method of transmission is through the ingestion of contaminated material such as feces.

## Pandemics

A pandemic is an epidemic of infectious disease that has spread through human populations across a large region, multiple continents, or even worldwide. Natural pandemics have killed more people than wars. However, natural pandemics are unlikely to be existential threats as there are usually some people resistant to the pathogen, and the offspring of survivors would be more resistant.

Nevertheless, a pandemic can occur on a scale which crosses international boundaries, usually affecting a large number of people. A pandemic usually starts with the virus infecting animals, and then moves to where the virus begins to spread directly between people, and accelerates when infections from the new virus have spread worldwide. The phases are of a pandemic defined by the spread of the disease, with accompanying mortality. Additional factors that can make a pandemic worse are resistance to antibiotic medicines, hemorrhagic fevers, and severe respiratory problems like pneumonia. The economic cost of a pandemic can be in the billions of dollars due to shutdowns in trade, travel, manufacturing and business transactions.

# Nuclear Waste Accumulation

## Overview

An immediate problem is the accumulation of tons of radioactive nuclear waste in the form of spent fuel by the production of energy in the many nuclear fission power plants that exist around the world. *The storage of these wastes in specially designed casks has produced a radioactive equivalent of over 2 million Hiroshima type bombs—an amount that can adversely affect the environment for over 300 generations if these casks were to leak.* Radiation and waste material such as plutonium from nuclear power sources are threats to human health, in particular, cancer—something that can occur in the process all the way from the initial uranium mining to the eventual nuclear power plant operation. Even if nothing more were to be added or done, the long-term results from the fallout of all nuclear devices that have been detonated by testing by the nuclear countries will produce an estimated one million or more cancer fatalities over the next century.

## Nuclear Weapons Waste

Nuclear weapons proliferation has created tons of uranium and plutonium waste materials. The concern is that if radioactive waste is stored in deep geological storage, over many years the fission products will seep into underground water systems. As time passes, these deep storage areas have the potential to decay and become uranium and plutonium mines that can be accessed by nations wanting to create nuclear weapons. Waste from the decommissioning of nuclear weapons adds to the radioactive materials that must be disposed of. Medical and industrial waste is another source that must be dealt with. High-level waste from nuclear reactors is still another large source of radioactive waste. All of these nuclear wastes must be disposed of to keep them from interacting with the biosphere.

In the United States at the Hanford, Washington nuclear facility during its time of operation from the 1940s until it was shut down in 1988, about 64 metric tons of plutonium were produced to create thousands of nuclear warheads. In the process, over 53 million gallons of radioactive waste were produced that were stored in 177 underground tanks—about one-third of which have deteriorated and leaked. About 450 billion gallons of additional radioactive liquid waste seeped into the ground, which has contaminated about 80 square miles of aquifers—some of which have trickled into the Columbia River. 8 million tons of contaminated trash have been collected and buried in a two-square-mile dump area. There are numerous species of insects and animals such as wasps, birds, ants, gophers and fruit flies that have been contaminated as well as plants such as tumbleweeds. Local cows were irradiated with radioactive iodine, and they passed this on through the milk that was produced from these herds.

# The Myth of Clean Coal

## Overview

There is plenty of evidence that the amount of carbon dioxide in the earth's atmosphere is increasing rapidly as a result of the combustion of fossil fuels. If the future rate of increase continues, it has been predicted that, because the CO2 envelope that reduces radiation is increasing, the temperature of the earth's atmosphere will also increase and that vast changes in the climates of the earth will result. Such changes in temperature will cause the melting of the polar icecaps, which, in turn, would result in the inundation of many coastal cities, including New York, Miami and London.

There are climate change deniers that argue that CO2 is a benign gas that is essential for all life. They maintain that while the benefits of CO2 are "proven", the alleged risks of climate change are based on speculation, and that they lack an adequate scientific basis. They state that coal is essential to affordable, reliable energy and that it will continue to play a significant role in the global energy mix for the foreseeable future. Their view of the coal technology is that it is vital to advancing global climate change solutions, and that the support of advanced coal technologies is one of continuous improvement toward the ultimate goal of near-zero emissions from coal—the "clean coal" scenario.

## The Myth

The myth of "clean coal" can be described as follows:

- Coal combustion releases the greenhouse gases CO2 and nitrous oxide (N2O) during combustion. Coal-fired power plants release more greenhouse gases per unit of energy produced than any other electricity source.
- Coal supplies 33% of the energy used for electricity in the United States, which makes coal-fired power plants a prime target for reducing greenhouse gas emissions.
- Coal is not economical and coal-fired plants are closing down throughout the United States as the fuel becomes less profitable due to state and federal regulations, an aging fleet and competition from other energy sectors such as wind and solar power.
- The coal mining process releases methane, which is 87 times more potent as a greenhouse gas than CO2.
- Carbon capture and storage technologies have been marketed as a way to address climate emissions from burning coal, by pumping CO2 produced through burning coal underground instead of into the air. However, the technology is extremely expensive, and even if the carbon can be sequestered, the coal-fired plant will still result in destructive coal mining and toxic coal ash as a byproduct.
- Coal combustion releases sulfur dioxide (SO2) and nitrogen oxides (NOx), which react with water and oxygen to form acid rain. Acid rain corrodes buildings and structures and acidifies freshwater environments, damaging aquatic ecosystems.

- Volatile organic compounds react to form ground-level ozone, or smog. Smog can cause a variety of respiratory and cardiovascular effects and is especially dangerous to the elderly, young children, and people with asthma.
- Fine particulate matter is released into the air in the form of fly ash. This particulate matter gets lodged in the lungs when inhaled and increases the risk for pulmonary diseases, including lung cancer.
- Coal-fired power plants account for 41% of anthropogenic (human-caused) mercury emissions, which can travel long distances before being deposited in soil or water. Mercury accumulates in food-chains and can reach very high levels in many types of fish that are consumed by humans. Mercury is highly toxic and is especially dangerous to children.
- Coal combustion waste contains many toxic chemicals and heavy metals, which are known to cause birth defects, reproductive disorders, neurological damage, learning disabilities, kidney disease, and diabetes.
- This coal waste is often stored in large impoundment ponds. Massive spills from breaches in these ponds have occurred, and many ponds are currently classified as a "high hazard" by the EPA. They are at risk to spill and will cause significant property damage, environmental damage, injuries and deaths.
- Impoundment ponds are known to leach contaminants like arsenic into the soil and groundwater, potentially poisoning freshwater sources.

# The Problem with Oil

## Overview

Petroleum is one of the main sources of energy in the world. Petroleum and its by-products are used to fuel various forms of transportation, industry and domestic electricity use. Petroleum is used to manufacture plastics, which provide products essential for daily life such as cosmetics, tires, and pesticides. Over the years there have been increased concerns over the negative environmental effects of the petroleum industry. This is due to the toxicity of petroleum which contributes to air pollution, acid rain and various illnesses in humans. Petroleum also fuels climate change due to the increased greenhouse gas emissions in its extraction, refinement, transport and consumption phases.

## Toxicity

Petroleum is a complex mixture of many hydrocarbon components. The toxicity of oils lies in the toxicity of each individual component of oil at the water solubility of that component and its lack of biodegradability. Different oils and petroleum-related products have different levels of toxicity. Levels of toxicity are influenced by many factors such as weathering, solubility and chemical properties such as persistence. Increased weathering tends to decrease levels of toxicity. Highly soluble substances tend to have higher levels of toxicity, with some oils having higher levels of toxicity such as benzene, which has the highest level of toxicity. Other substances which are highly toxic include toluene, methylbenzene and xylenes.

Despite varying levels of toxicity amongst different variants of oil, all petroleum-derived products have adverse impacts on human health and the ecosystem. Oil emulsions in digestive systems in certain mammals result in decreased ability to digest nutrients that include capillary ruptures and hemorrhages, which lead to death. Ecosystem food chains are affected due to a decrease in algae productivity, threatening certain species. Oil is very lethal to fish, which it kills quickly. The toxicity of petroleum related products also threatens human health. Many compounds found in oil are highly toxic and can cause cancer as well as other diseases. Crude oil and petroleum distillates can cause birth defects and premature births. Benzene is known to cause leukemia in humans. The compound is also known to lower the white blood cell count in humans, which leaves people exposed to it more susceptible to infections. Hodgkin's lymphoma and other blood and immune system diseases can occur from exposure to benzene.

## Air Pollution

Emissions from the petroleum industry occur in every chain of the oil-producing process from the extraction to the consumption phase. In the extraction phase there are emissions of CO2 and other pollutants like nitrous oxides and aerosols as well as by-products like carbon monoxide and methanol. When oil or petroleum distillates are combusted, the combustion is not complete and the chemical reaction leaves other by-products. The refinement stages of petroleum contribute to large amounts of pollution in urban areas.

The increase in air pollution has adverse effects on human health due to the toxicity of oil. There is an increased occurrence of premature births in mothers that live in close proximity to oil refineries. There are also differences observed in sex ratios and the birth weight of children. Fine particulates of soot, which is a carcinogenic substance, blacken human lungs and cause heart problems or death.

Acid Rain

The combustion process of petroleum is responsible for much of the increased occurrence of acid rain. Petroleum combustion causes an increased amount of nitrous oxides, along with sulfur dioxide from the sulfur in the oil. These petroleum by-products combine with water in the atmosphere to create acid rain, and have produced increases in nitrous oxide emissions, which have significant effects on the pH levels of rainfall. The acid rain has adverse impacts on the larger ecosystem, such as killing trees, killing fish by acidifying lakes, and destroying coral reefs. Acid rain leads to the corrosion of machinery and structures, and to the slow destruction of archeological structures like marble ruins.

Rainwater in some parts of the United States contains high enough levels of potentially toxic substances such as PFAS that can affect human health, and may be found in drinking water. PFAS appear in an array of everyday items, such as food packaging, clothing and carpeting. The number of different PFAS variants are more than 4,700, but federal regulations only target two of them. Some of these chemicals have been known to cause serious health issues such as cancer, immune system deficiencies and thyroid problems. There is widespread PFAS contamination of the nation's lakes, rivers and groundwater reserves, which could also be ubiquitous in rain. PFAS chemicals are entering rainwater through a variety of avenues, like direct industrial emissions and evaporation. More rainwater research is needed, especially as to what we are inhaling and ingesting from PFAS.

Climate Change

The combustion of petroleum causes an increased amount of $CO_2$ emissions as well as other greenhouse gases. An increase of $CO_2$ results in an increase in surface temperatures. The combustion of petroleum for transport, industrial and domestic use is one of the major forms of $CO_2$ air pollution. The ultimate byproduct of oil combustion, which is $CO_2$, is accompanied by other by-products such as carbon monoxide and nitrates. These byproducts react with the atmosphere to produce ozone and other greenhouse gases. The increased pollution has consequences on global temperature. The atmosphere reflects 30% of the incoming longwave radiation back and keeps 70% of it for warmth. An increased carbon dioxide concentration in the atmosphere acts as a blanket for increased heat as more longwave radiation is trapped in the atmosphere. When there is a higher concentration of $CO_2$, this trapping results in increased surface temperatures. The climate system will heat up by 3 degrees Celsius for every doubling of

CO2. The warming of the temperatures will have massive impacts on rainfall patterns, retreat of glaciers, and sea levels, which will affect coastal communities.

## Oil Spills

An oil spill is the release of liquid petroleum hydrocarbons into the environment due to human activity, which causes pollution, especially in marine areas. Marine oil spills, where oil is released into the ocean or coastal waters are the most common, but oil spills may occur on land. Oil spills may be due to releases of crude oil from oil tankers, pipelines, railcars, offshore platforms, drilling rigs and wells, as well as spills of refined petroleum products, such as gasoline or diesel, and their by-products, such as heavier fuels used by large ships like bunker fuel or the spill of any oily refuse or waste oil.

Major oil spills that have occurred include the Exxon Valdez oil tanker in Prince William Sound, Alaska in 1989; the Lakeview Gusher in Kern County, California in 1910; the Gulf War oil spill in Kuwait in 1991; and the Deepwater Horizon oil spill in the Gulf of Mexico in 2010. Spilt oil penetrates into the structure of the plumage of birds and the fur of mammals, reducing its insulating ability, and making them more vulnerable to temperature fluctuations and much less buoyant in the water. Cleanup and recovery from an oil spill is difficult and depends upon many factors, including the type of oil spilled, the temperature of the water, which affects evaporation and biodegradation, and the types of shorelines and beaches that are involved. Other factors influencing the rate of long-term contamination is the continuous inputs of petroleum residues, and the rate at which the environment can clean itself. Oil spills may take weeks, months or even years to clean up.

## Waste Products

Volatile organic compounds are gases or vapors that are emitted by various solids and liquids. Petroleum hydrocarbons such as gasoline, diesel, or jet fuel intruding into indoor spaces from underground storage tanks threaten safety because of their explosive potential, and which can cause adverse health effects from inhalation. Waste oil contains breakdown products and impurities. When waste oil from vehicles drips out from engines over streets and roads, the oil travels into the water table bringing with it toxins such as benzene. This poisons the soil and drinking water when runoff from storms carries waste oil into rivers and oceans.

## Natural Gas is Not the Answer

Natural gas is marketed as a clean energy source. But the reality is very different than the marketing. Natural gas is a highly polluting fossil fuel. Its impacts include the following:

- While natural gas is a cleaner burning resource than coal and liquid petroleum, it emits a large amount of carbon into the atmosphere in the form of CO2 and methane.
- CO2 is released during natural gas combustion, which is the process that is used to generate electricity.
- Methane is leaked in large quantities during extraction and transport of natural gas, and is a greenhouse gas that is 87 time more potent than CO2.
- Global methane emissions have spiked dramatically since 2002 due to the boom in natural gas extraction in the United States. Leaked methane cancels out any reduction in CO2 emissions brought about by replacing coal with natural gas.
- When natural gas leaks at extraction sites, pollutants such as volatile organic compounds are emitted into the atmosphere. These pollutants react to form ground-level ozone, or smog, which can cause a variety of respiratory and cardiovascular effects and which is especially dangerous to the elderly, young children, and people with asthma.
- Diesel fumes from the operation of trucks and machinery and gas leaks on drill sites pose a hazard to workers and nearby residents. People who live near areas of high oil and gas activity have been found to be at risk for chronic illness and cancer.
- Hydraulic fracturing, also known as fracking, is a process by which natural gas is extracted from wells. Fracking is a dangerous practice due to the following:
    - Depending on location and well-type, fracking can use between 1.5 and 15.8 million gallons of water per well.
    - Wastewater from these wells is often disposed of by injecting it deep underground into injection wells. These wells can cause earthquakes in the surrounding area. This puts people and buildings at risk, and increases the potential for groundwater contamination with wastewater.
    - Accidents or poorly built wells can lead to contamination of groundwater by additives in the fracking fluid. These additives can contain dangerous chemicals such as benzene and lead, which are toxic to humans.
    - Extraction companies are not required to disclose all the components of fracking fluid. Many components are considered "trade secrets" and are never reported to regulatory agencies.
    - Naturally occurring radioactive materials often come to the surface where they can build up in wastewater pipes. This can lead to maintenance workers being exposed to higher levels of radiation.

# No More Nuclear Fission Plants

Green America is active in addressing the climate crisis by transitioning the United States electricity production away from its heavy emphasis on coal-fired and natural gas power. But, if we transition from fossil fuels to an equally dangerous source, that of nuclear power, it is not a viable solution. It may produce lower-carbon energy, but this energy comes with a great deal of risk. We have already experienced the Chernobyl, Three-Mile Island and Fukushima Daiichi nuclear disasters that show just how dangerous a nuclear power plant can be when something goes wrong.

Currently there are 444 nuclear power plants in 30 countries worldwide, with another 63 plants under construction. Those nuclear fission plants should not be built for the following reasons:

- The waste generated by nuclear reactors remains radioactive for tens to hundreds of thousands of years. Currently, there are no long-term storage solutions for radioactive waste, and most is stored in temporary, above-ground facilities. These facilities are running out of storage space, so the nuclear industry is turning to other types of storage that are costlier and potentially less safe.
- There is great concern that the development of nuclear energy programs increases the likelihood of proliferation of nuclear weapons. As nuclear fuel and technologies become globally available, the risk of these falling into the wrong hands is a threat. To avoid proliferation, it is important that countries with corruption and instability be discouraged from creating nuclear programs.
- Nuclear power plants are a potential target for terrorist operations. An attack could cause major explosions, putting population centers at risk, as well as ejecting dangerous radioactive material into the atmosphere and surrounding region. Nuclear research facilities, uranium enrichment plants, and uranium mines are potentially at risk for attacks that could cause widespread contamination with radioactive material.
- Human error and natural disasters can lead to dangerous and costly accidents. The 1986 Chernobyl disaster in Ukraine led to the deaths of employees and nearby residents with the explosion, and has had a variety of negative health effects on thousands of people. A massive tsunami bypassed the safety mechanisms of several power plants in 2011, causing three nuclear meltdowns at a power plant in Fukushima, Japan that resulted in the release of radioactive materials into the surrounding area. In both disasters, hundreds of thousands of people were relocated, millions of dollars were spent, and the radiation-related deaths are still being experienced. Cancer rates among populations living in proximity to Chernobyl and Fukushima, especially among children, rose significantly in the years after the accidents. Even the Three-Mile Island partial meltdown of a nuclear reactor resulted in the release of radioactive gases and radioactive iodine into the environment.
- In addition to the significant risk of cancer associated with fallout from nuclear disasters, there is an increased risk for those who reside near a nuclear power plant, especially for childhood cancers such as leukemia. Workers in the nuclear

industry are exposed to higher than normal levels of radiation, and are at risk of death from cancer at a rate similar to the that of Japanese nuclear bomb survivors

- The 444 nuclear power plants currently in existence provide about 11% of the world's energy. In order to meet current and future energy needs, the nuclear sector would have to scale up to 14,500 plants. Uranium, the fuel for nuclear reactors, is energy-intensive to mine, and deposits discovered in the future are likely to be harder to get to. Much of the net energy created by nuclear power plants would be offset by the energy input required to build and decommission plants, and to mine and process uranium ore. Any reduction in greenhouse gas emissions brought about by switching from coal to nuclear power is negligible.
- Scaling up to 14,500 nuclear plants is not possible due to the limitation of feasible sites. Nuclear plants need to be located near a source of water for cooling, and there aren't enough locations in the world that are safe from droughts, flooding, hurricanes, earthquakes, or other potential disasters that could trigger a nuclear accident. The increase in extreme weather events only compounds this risk.
- Nuclear costs are on the rise, and many plants are being shut down or are in danger of being shut down for economic reasons. Initial capital costs, fuel, and maintenance costs are much higher for nuclear power plants than wind, and nuclear projects tend to suffer cost overruns and construction delays.
- Investment in nuclear plants, security, mining infrastructure, and waste disposal draws funding away from investment in cleaner sources such as wind, solar, and geothermal. Financing for renewable energy is already scarce, and increasing nuclear capacity will only add to the competition for funding.
- Going down the nuclear route would mean that poor countries that do not have the financial resources to invest in and develop nuclear power, would become reliant on rich, technologically advanced nations. But, poor nations without experience in the building and maintaining of nuclear plants may decide to build them anyway. Countries with a history of nuclear power use have learned the importance of regulation, oversight, and investment in safety when it comes to nuclear. A world that is more reliant on nuclear power would involve many plants in countries that have little experience with nuclear energy, no regulatory background in the field and questionable records on quality control, safety and corruption.

# Genetic Engineering

## Overview

Genetic manipulation of organisms through the splicing of DNA genes from one species into the DNA genes of another species is a technique that is largely unknown and is fraught with potential dangers with respect to its consequences to human health and the environment. Dangerous health problems may result as plant, animal, bacteria and viruses are manipulated in ways that they do not naturally exist—and through genes which can even be synthesized in the laboratory in arrangements that do not exist in nature. Living organisms exist in the world as a result of millions of years of natural evolution of life. Crossing these natural boundaries constitutes tampering with the evolution of all species. It could result in the creation of new organisms—including those of rogue toxins, enhanced allergens, altered viruses and new forms of bacteria, which may result in the introduction of new diseases and the spread of epidemics and pandemics caused by unstable gene combinations.

## The Alteration of Genetic Codes

The alteration of genetic codes may interfere with crops and proteins in unpredictable ways, with a potential to create a catastrophic effect on the ecosystem. Potentially harmful genetic transmutations involve the creation of "terminator" seeds, the development of foods with less or different nutritional values, and the cloning of animals such as cows, pigs and chickens. In some genetic tampering animal eggs are mixed with human genes to create human-animal embryos, presumably for research into diseases such as Parkinson's disorder, AIDS, Alzheimer's syndrome and arthritis. These cells have the potential to become any tissue, and can create new hybrid forms of life. Its most extreme form is the connection of machine elements with living cells—such as with prosthetic devices—but which are theoretically possible to produce bionic entities, with goals of creating the perfect soldier, the compliant robotic worker, a highly-gifted individual with advanced traits, and other types of special beings.

DNA sequences involve very complex and interrelated systems. If these are altered in an adverse manner by random mutations, they are capable of producing environmental disasters on an unprecedented scale. Genetically engineered bacteria have already been used for almost three decades to manufacture processed foods—merely to generate more product at less cost—and without doing any significant testing as to effects. Genetically modified medicines may adversely affect human health by the introduction of unknown side effects such as in vaccines or other injections. The primary problem with genetically modified organisms is that *once they are released into the environment, they will remain in the gene pool of a species—or pass between species—for countless generations, with hidden harmful effects that may not become evident until much later.*

# Overconsumption

## Overview

The world's population has consumed more goods in the last 50 years than what was consumed by all previous generations who have ever existed on earth. This conspicuous consumption has had an effect on energy—especially oil—as well as on timber and steel. It is a lopsided activity since the developed nations consume many times more than the developing and undeveloped nations. The world's richest one-fifth of the population consumes 90% of all goods and services, over 80% of all commercial energy that is produced, and 50% of all meat and fish that are brought to market. One-half of the world's countries that contain three-fourths of the world's population use less than one-fifth of the commercial energy that is produced—and only cause one-half of the pollution that the richest nations emit into the environment.

## Energy Impact

The material requirements for production in our modern industrial economies are enormous as are the environmental impacts of the consumption of these products. In the industrialized societies, an average person consumes many tons of raw materials each year, all of which must be extracted, processed, and ultimately disposed of as wastes. Commercial energy produced by coal, oil and nuclear fuels is part of this consumption and equally affects the environment. The energy impact comes from taking resources from the earth, then changing them into usable products, and then consuming them. During this entire process various wastes are produced, and they are often released into the air, land and water environments as pollution.

## Cost Factor

There is a definite cost factor that is associated with over consumption. The dramatic increase in the price of oil and of other commodities is indicative of a combination of reduced resources and increased demand. It represents resource consumption that cannot be sustained indefinitely at the current rates of consumption. This situation is emphasized by the oceans in which large proportions of the world's fish stocks have already been overfished—some perhaps terminally. There are too many fishing boats chasing too few fish, with the price of some varieties of fish increasing to unprecedented levels.

The current imbalance between resources and population prevents a sustainable living on the planet. This imbalance has been created by following bad policies, which in turn have resulted in major environmental and survival problems. It is not just population increases that threaten the environment, but also the lack of access to resources by the poorest nations, and the over consumption of resources by the richest nations.

## The Effects

Overconsumption occurs when resource use outpaces the sustainable capacity of the ecosystem, which leads to environmental degradation and the loss of resources. An effect of overconsumption is a reduction in the planet's carrying capacity. Excessive and unsustainable consumption will exceed the long-term carrying capacity of its environment and will lead to subsequent resource depletion, environmental degradation and reduced ecological health. Overconsumption has enabled a new over class to exist, displaying symptoms of affluenza and showing a marked increase in obesity. In the long term these effects can lead to increased conflict over dwindling resources, and in the long run, a forced return to subsistence-level conditions once the population growth has outpaced agricultural production. The world's ecological capacity is insufficient to satisfy the ambitions and aspirations of every country in the world in a sustainable way.

## Consequences

Everything that we consume comes from the natural world, whether it is extracted, mined, farmed, grown, fished or cut down. Since the resources on this planet are limited, as we continue to consume at an ever-increasing rate, the planet suffers from this over-extraction of resources. The decimation of forests, overfishing, soil depletion, decreases in oil and water shortages all result in degraded and collapsing ecosystems, habitat loss and species extinction. Increased consumption creates increased pollution and waste such that air, land and water get more polluted and toxic.

When the majority share of the planet's resources is used up by a minority of the earth's population, then others have less to live on. These resources are exploited and used for producing goods and services for the minority of the world's population instead of being used to provide the basic necessities of shelter, food, water, health and sanitation for the rest of the world's population. the overconsumption by the rich minority results in precious resources being directed towards frivolous or luxury items, further depriving the poor of the world.

**Global Problems**

# Terrorism

Ever since the first World Trade Center bombing in 1993, America has been on heightened alert for foreign terrorism conducted within the United States. The lessons of 9-11 and other terror incidents have led to an increase in technology to detect and prevent such acts. Developing technologies combined with a good strategy requires technological investments in the following areas:

- Developing new technologies that can contribute to building a national system that addresses all the challenges of terrorism from intelligence and early warning to domestic counterterrorism and response. The first priority of a strategy should be to invest in technologies that best leverage all the existing capabilities that are available by integrating them into a cohesive system.
- Adopting technologies that get the most from investment is prudent because spending only a little for research, development, and procurement resources on many things may not produce much. Targeting investments on the technologies that can provide the most security for the resources invested, ones that are the most flexible, and ones that contribute to addressing a wide range of threats is a better approach in dealing with terrorists.
- Researching breakthrough technologies are need, which allow law enforcement officials to update their investigatory techniques or implement new security measures is the desired approach. The development of countermeasures against terrorism calls for unprecedented innovation.
- Using system integration technologies will result in getting the most out of the resources that are available. That means adopting a new approach to counterterrorism operations as well as the enabling technologies to support it. Network-centric operations generate increased operational effectiveness by networking sensors, decision makers, law enforcement officials, and emergency responders to achieve shared awareness, increased speed of command, higher tempo of operations, greater efficiency, increased security and safety, reduced vulnerability to potential hostile action, and a degree of self-synchronization. This involves linking knowledgeable entities from the local to the national levels in an integrated network that addresses counterterrorism missions ranging from intelligence and early warning to response and post-strike investigations and forensic analysis. The technologies that are required to facilitate network-centric counterterrorism operations include information technologies that facilitate passing high volumes of secure digital data. These create ad hoc networks, software that integrates disparate databases, and hardware that links various communication systems over cable, fiber-optic, wireless, and satellite networks.
- Biometrics for finding identities is the linchpin of all security and investigatory systems. Using biometrics for identity verification, especially in the areas of visa and immigration documentation and government-issued identification card programs is a definite requirement. Biometrics uses recorded measures of a unique physical or behavioral characteristic of individuals that can be used for verification or for identification by a process of matching that includes iris recognition, hand geometry, fingerprint recognition, face recognition, and voice

recognition. Some newer emerging technologies include vein scans, facial thermography, DNA matching, odor sensing, blood pulse measurements, skin pattern recognition, nail bed identification, gait recognition, and ear shape recognition.

- The use of non-lethal weapons may offer law enforcement a new range of options for taking the battle to the terrorists without endangering others. Non-lethal weapons are discriminate, explicitly designed and employed to incapacitate personnel or materiel while minimizing fatalities and undesired damage to property and the environment. These weapons are a set of capabilities, which have three functions:
    - Counter-personnel, which involves controlling crowds, incapacitating people, preventing access to specific areas, and removing people from facilities, buildings, or areas of operation
    - Counter-material, which involves preventing vehicles, vessels, or aircraft from entering an area or disabling or neutralizing these means of transportation
    - Counter-capabilities, which focuses on disabling or neutralizing facilities and systems

Non-lethal weapons technologies cover a broad spectrum, including areas related to acoustics systems, chemicals such as anti-traction materials, dyes, markers, calmatives and malodorants, communications systems, electromagnetic and electrical systems, entanglement and other mechanical systems, information technologies, optical devices, and non-penetrating projectiles and munitions. Other techniques include directed-energy systems, high-power microwave, solid-state lasers, marine barrier systems, and unmanned or remotely piloted platforms and other sensors for intelligence collection and assessments.

- Data mining and link analysis technologies can be used to analyze bills, license applications, visa forms, census records, and telephone lists. Rather than trying to narrow the scope of information that has to be looked at, data mining and link analysis technologies work by exploiting larger and larger amounts of information to identify patterns and anomalies from the observation of vast datasets to make predictions and descriptions. Prediction involves using some variables or fields in the database to predict unknown or future values of other variables of interest, and description focuses on finding human-interpretable patterns describing the data to find commonalities. Link analysis can be used to prevent a terrorist attack by understanding the relationships among individuals, organizations, and other entities, which could be security threats. Link analysis analyzes the data surrounding the suspect relationships to determine how they are connected. More research needs to be done to handle non-structured formats that are a mix of text, image, video, and sensor information.
- Nanotechnology involves developing or working with materials and complete systems at the atomic, molecular, or macromolecular levels. Research areas include materials, sensors, biomedical nanostructures, electronics, optics, and fabrication. Nano-scale sensors are designed to form a weak chemical bond to the substance of whatever is to be sensed, and then to change their properties in response. Biomedical nanostructures interact with people at the molecular level,

allowing for targeted drug delivery, adhesive materials for skin grafts or bandages, and so forth. Nano-scale electronics can help to shrink computer circuits even further and to make them more efficient. Nano-scale optics allow for materials that fluoresce to be tuned to change specific properties under certain conditions. Fabrication at the nanoscale offers the potential of creating devices from the atom up, instead of having to shrink materials down to the needed size. This includes semiconductor chips, bio-molecular devices, molecular electronics, integrated microsystems and micro-electrical-mechanical systems, smart systems-on-a-chip and microscale and nanoscale instrumentation, and measurement technologies.

- Directed energy weapons could provide counterterrorism protection for critical infrastructure. These include lasers and microwave radiation emitters, which can inflict casualties and damage equipment by depositing energy on their intended target. Directed energy weapons can hit a target with subatomic particles or electromagnetic waves to generate very high power beams that focus specifically and accurately on a target.

There are barriers to development of counterterrorism technology. The biggest one is cost as not enough money is being spent to develop these capabilities. Another factor is technology risk that techniques may not perform as expected or turn out to be inadequate for the tasks. Human reluctance to develop these technologies also plays a part, primarily due to concerns of decreasing civil liberties, legal challenges, and the task of safeguarding the technology so that it doesn't fall into terrorists' hands. But, with enough foresight, it will be possible to increase the methods of counterterrorism to new and yet comfortable levels that do not impede the civil liberties of American citizens.

# Nuclear Proliferation

## The Armament Race

During WWII, three other nations besides the United States were involved in nuclear research with the aim of developing an atomic weapon: Germany, Japan and the Soviet Union. Germany constructed a nuclear pile at Haigerloch near the Black Forest where Werner Heisenberg, Otto Han, Carl von Weizsacker, Max von Laue and others were working with heavy water and high-quality uranium ore. Japan constructed a preliminary gaseous diffusion experiment by Yoshio Nishina at Riken near Tokyo. The Soviet Union pursued the acquisition of the atom bomb with the work headed by Igor Kurchatov at a research facility located in Sarov, and by an active espionage effort of the nuclear research that was conducted at Los Alamos, New Mexico.

General Groves ordered the refurbishment of the Los Alamos Laboratory, which was followed by a presidential executive order to make the site a permanent location for conducting research on atomic bombs as well as for more powerful weapons—like the hydrogen bomb—and for applications of atomic energy for peaceful purposes. In 1947, control of the Los Alamos Laboratory was transferred to the United States Atomic Energy Commission (AEC). Teller and other scientists such as Bethe, Fermi and Lawrence became consultants, and Oppenheimer was appointed to serve on the AEC as part of the General Advisory Committee along with others such as Conant, Rabi and Fermi to advise General Groves in the development of nuclear weapons. Dr. Lawrence recommended that the United States pursue plant expansions to build up a sizable stock of nuclear bombs for military use.

In 1953, President Dwight Eisenhower addressed the United Nations in a speech called "Atoms for Peace", which was aimed at the reduction of the threat from nuclear weapons, and the development of peaceful applications of atomic energy. However, other countries joined the nuclear weapons club, ending the United States monopoly on atomic weapons:

- In 1949, the Soviet Union exploded its first atomic bomb
- In 1952, Great Britain conducted its first test of an atomic bomb
- In 1955, the Soviet Union exploded its first hydrogen bomb[13]
- In 1957, Great Britain conducted its first test of a hydrogen bomb
- In 1960, France tested its first atomic bomb
- In 1964, China carried out its first atomic bomb test
- In 1967, China exploded its first hydrogen bomb
- In 1968, France detonated a hydrogen bomb
- In 1974, India conducted its first atomic bomb test
- In 1978, Pakistan exploded its first atomic bomb
- In 1998, India detonated a small-scale hydrogen bomb
- In 2006, North Korea tested its first atomic bomb
- In 2016, North Korea tested its first hydrogen bomb

The three Soviet Union successor states that inherited nuclear arsenals (Ukraine, Kazakhstan, and Belarus) relinquished all their nuclear warheads, which were removed to Russia. South Africa's apartheid regime built six nuclear bombs but dismantled them later. Argentina began a nuclear weapons program, but abolished it in 1983. Brazil had intended to build nuclear weapons, but dismantled the project in 1990. Sweden considered plans for building nuclear weapons, but scrapped all plans in the 1970s. Israel created both atom bombs and hydrogen bombs since the 1970s, but has never acknowledged their existence.

Iraq's nuclear reactor research center was started in 1977 by President Saddam Hussein for the purpose of creating nuclear weapons. In 1980, an Iranian air strike damaged the site, and in 1981, Israel finished crippling the site with an air attack. In 1991, the site was completely destroyed by American aircraft during the Gulf War. In 2007, Israeli aircraft raided a Syrian cache of nuclear materials and destroyed buildings in which personnel were engaged in constructing a nuclear arsenal with the help of North Korea.

Currently, Iran is intensifying its research towards the goal of developing an atomic weapon. In 2011, Saudi Arabia was reported as having bought two nuclear bombs from Pakistan for use in their own defense. In view of Iran's capability to develop a nuclear weapon, Saudi Arabia is considering developing nuclear weapons.

The world's nuclear nations collectively possess over 30,000 nuclear weapon devices, which represent more than one million Hiroshimas in destructive capability—and more than enough to wipe out every living species on earth. The global threat of nuclear weapons continues to increase dramatically, and is of much concern with the possibility of terrorists—or rogue nations—acquiring these weapons. The acquisition of nuclear devices by terrorists will make cities and countries subject to attacks that could conceivably kill thousands and affect millions of people through radiation damage.

Many efforts have been started to curtail the increase in atomic weapons, but so far none has produced any meaningful agreements. An ABM treaty between the United States and the Soviet Union was abrogated. A Non-Proliferation Treaty has not met with much success. Other non-proliferation efforts have been the Cooperative Threat reduction program, the Global Threat Reduction Initiative, the proliferation Security Initiative and the Additional Protocols Initiative. The result of these failures has made the world a more dangerous place, and so new efforts have been started to reduce the number of stockpiled nuclear weapons in both the United States and Russia.

In 1969, President Nixon offered to hold negotiations with the Soviet government, which became the Strategic Arms Limitation Talks (SALT). In 1972, these talks resulted in the Anti-Ballistic Missile Treaty between the Soviet Union and the United States. However, the treaty was never ratified by the Senate. In 1982, President Reagan abandoned SALT and began the Strategic Arms Reduction Treaty (START) talks. In 1991, the Soviet Union and the United States signed the START I Treaty to reduce the number of nuclear weapons. Another treaty, START II, was ratified by the United States Senate—but not by the Russian Duma, their representative assembly. In 2002, the Treaty of Moscow was signed by both countries to reduce each of their nuclear arsenals by about two-thirds: from 6,000 to 2,200 by 2012. In 2010, President Barack Obama and President Dmitry Medvedev of Russia signed the new START treaty to reduce the number of nuclear weapons in each of their arsenals, which the Senate approved in 2010. The treaty calls for reducing the number of warheads to 1,500 and the number of launchers to 700. However, President Trump has abandoned all of these efforts and is concentrating on the development of small tactical nuclear weapons.

## Dealing with the Consequences

In 1950, Neils Bohr presented a letter to the United Nations stating his concern with a nuclear arms race. He called for a free exchange of nuclear information among all countries of the world to promote a peaceful cooperation between nations. In 1955, Bertrand Russell and Albert Einstein collaborated in writing a manifesto warning about the consequences of a nuclear war, and that it was a matter of either renouncing war altogether—or else face the possibility of eliminating the human race from the planet. They stated that it was a choice of either opening up a new paradise on earth, or risking universal death.

Since the 1950s, the threat of a nuclear war has escalated. A recent call for reducing and eventually eliminating nuclear weapons was issued by a letter published in the *Wall Street Journal* in 2007 that was authored by George Schultz, Henry Kissinger, William Perry and Sam Nunn. The letter warned that the world has grown more dangerous with the rise of an increasing number of nuclear nations, and they advocated a move towards the reduction and eventual elimination of nuclear weapons.

Former Russian Premier Mikhail Gorbachev shared the same vision and published a letter in the *Wall Street Journal* that warned that the possession of nuclear weapons would ultimately lead to their use as an acceptable means of fighting wars. He cited the inherent danger of these being used in a pre-emptive strike against another country, making it a weapon of genocide. An all-out nuclear war would be the worst scenario as it would cause a nuclear winter, probably destroy the ozone layer, create widespread epidemics, result in mass starvations because of the disruptions in food transport, and possibly produce a nuclear spring that would wipe out crops. The worst outcome would be the annihilation of human beings from earth.

# Increasing Population

## Overview

The greatest single force, which is behind most of the present world crisis, is that of overpopulation. The world's population is growing exponentially and is expected to reach 8 billion by 2023, 9 billion by 2040, and 10 billion by 2055. This population time bomb keeps ticking away, straining all of the resources of the planet, overburdening health facilities, creating circumstances for diseases to thrive in, adding to the famine and hunger conditions that already exist, and worsening the unstable and volatile situations, which are presently undergoing a series of social, economic and political upheavals. By 2100, we will have nearly seven times more people on this planet than we did in 1900 (1.5 billion)—with all of them competing for the same food, water and habitation space. The earth could probably handle this number of people—*but only if the population and resources were evenly distributed*. The underlying problem is that the majority of the earth's population is accumulated in the urban centers, with the most persons being located in the poorest developing nations. These highly concentrated populations are becoming a form of permanent centers of urban decay, with a flourishing illegal drug trade and an associated high rate of crime due to breakdowns in law and civil order, along with urban congestion and noise.

## Population Growth

The population growth has been explosive in the last seven decades as the number of people has tripled from 2.5 billion in 1950 to more than 7.7 billion in 2020. The overall effect of this accelerated growth has been on living standards. The related resource use and depletion, and its effect on the earth's environment will continue to make itself felt with greater criticality in the coming years. Because of the large and increasing population size, the total number of people added to the global population will remain high for several decades—*even if growth rates decline*. Even if a stable population growth level is achieved, the resource consumption will still continue to rise because of economic growth.

Population growth has the most impact in countries that appear least able to deal with its consequences. Key issues in providing for increased populations in these nations include the achievement of adequate income levels, food availability, national security, employment, and the provision of basic social services. The lack of beneficial management of natural resources affects the livelihoods of a majority of their inhabitants. In many of these areas, the population growth is accelerating the rate of degradation of forests, fisheries, drinking water and productive soils. The situation is compounded because most of these people already live in absolute poverty, are undernourished and are illiterate.

Population growth, together with continued economic expansion, presents additional risks at the global level. If the world's population continues to increase, and incomes also continue to rise—even if only slightly—then it is likely that the production and consumption patterns characteristic of income groups in the developed nations will be emulated throughout the developing world. The environmental impacts of this increased economic activity that will be required to support modern consumer societies are already immense, especially in the provision of food, clothing, shelter, transportation and energy. If the consumers of the future use and waste resources in the same manner as those of present era in developed countries, then the consequences in terms of global climate change, loss of vital renewable resources, and toxic pollution will be very severe.

The human population has been growing since the end of 1400, but the most significant increase has been in the last 50 years. The most optimistic estimate for the carrying capacity of the earth is a maximum of 16,000,000,000 people. As of 2020, the world population figure stood at 7,770,000,000. Environmental problems, such as rising levels of atmospheric carbon dioxide, global warming and pollution are aggravated by the population explosion. Other problems associated with overpopulation include the increased demand for resources such as fresh water and food, starvation, malnutrition, over-consumption of natural resources, waste and a deterioration in the quality of life, especially in living conditions.

It may be that overpopulation has already occurred, especially in terms of depletion of natural resources, degradation of the environment, the numerous conflicts and wars, the rise in unemployment, the high cost of living, entrenched poverty, the lack of fresh water, lower life expectancy, democratic freedom decline, elevated crime rates, harmful impacts on agriculture, habitat loss, global warming and climate change, the occurrence of new epidemics and pandemics, species extinction, global warming and climate change.

# Food Shortages

## Overview

About one billion people on earth are undernourished, and about one-third of all nations cannot grow or buy enough food to sustain their populations. More than 6 billion people die each year due to malnutrition. 10% of the world's farmlands and 70% of the world's rangelands are degraded—a situation that affects both grain and meat production.

## Malnutrition and Starvation

Malnutrition is the underlying cause of more than one-half of all child deaths, and poor nourishment leaves the surviving children underweight and weakened. The undernourishment does not have to be severe to have a significant impact on child health and survival. As soon as their immunity systems are compromised, the result can be that usually non-fatal illnesses—such as diarrhea, dysentery, pneumonia, malaria and measles—can kill them.

More people are starving due to induced disasters such as wars, civil strife, land degradation and economic crises in which humans play a role in all food shortages, which are exacerbated by natural causes of drought and flooding, by the accelerating greenhouse effect, by the erosion of 75% of the topsoil, and by the hole in the ozone layer. Because huge numbers of animals are now concentrated in feedlots, confinement buildings and factory farms, their wastes are not being returned to the soil, but are instead being washed into the water systems. This not only pollutes the water, but it removes the nutrients that are used for crops—making the soil less fertile.

## The Food Crisis

The basic facts of the food crisis are these:

- 98% of people suffering from hunger live in developing countries where 13% of the population is undernourished.
- 66 million primary school-age children attend classes hungry across the developing world.
- Hunger kills more people every year than AIDS, malaria and tuberculosis combined.
- 17 million children are born underweight annually, the result of inadequate nutrition before and during pregnancy.
- 5 million children die each year due to hunger.
- One-fourth of the world's children are stunted in growth due to poor nutrition.
- One seventh of the world's population is undernourished.

The world needs to produce at least 50% more food to feed the 9 billion people that are expected to be the population of earth by 2040. But, climate change could cut crop yields by more than 25%. The land, biodiversity, oceans, forests, and other forms of natural capital are being depleted at unprecedented rates. Unless we change how we grow our food and manage our natural capital, food security—especially for the world's poorest—will be at risk.

High food prices are causing many poor families to cope by pulling their children out of school so they won't have to pay for their school lunches. These families are also eating cheaper and less nutritious food, which can have severe life-long effects on the social, physical, and mental well-being of millions of young people. Malnutrition contributes to infant, child, and maternal illness, and causes decreased learning capacity, lower productivity, and higher mortality.

## Global Warming Effect of Food production

Global warming is being created by human activity and is threatening to disrupt global food supplies. Human-caused greenhouse gas causes climate change and climate volatility and it's going to stress the agricultural supply chain. Climate change is going to make it extremely difficult to feed the world's growing population. Extreme weather and the decline in pollinating insects are already impacting food production. Climate change will place stress on vulnerable growing regions around the world that provide important ingredients to make foods such as cocoa, vanilla and almonds where:

- 70% of the world's cocoa is sourced from two countries in West Africa.
- 90% of the world's vanilla is sourced from Madagascar.
- 80% of the world's almonds are grown in California.

Any disruptions to these three areas would devastate these three specific foodstuffs.

# Lack of Fresh Water

## Overview

75% of Earth is covered in water of which 97% of that is ocean and only 3% of that is fresh water. 70% of this freshwater is in the form of glaciers and ice caps, with the remaining 30% being land surface water such as rivers, lakes, ponds and groundwater. Most of the fresh water resources are either unreachable or too polluted, leaving less than 1% of the world's fresh water, or about 0.003% of all the water on earth, readily accessible for direct human use. Fresh water—what we drink, bathe in, and irrigate our farm fields with—is incredibly rare.

Water scarcity in due to the failure of institutions to ensure a regular supply, or due to a lack of an adequate infrastructure. Water scarcity already affects every continent as water use has been growing globally at more than twice the rate of population increase. An increasing number of regions are reaching the limit at which water services can be sustainably delivered, especially in arid regions. Water scarcity will be exacerbated as rapidly growing urban areas place heavy pressure on neighboring water resources. Climate change and bio-energy demands are expected to amplify the already complex relationship between world development and water demand.

## Water Usage

One-half of all fresh water on earth is currently being used by people—a process that is causing aquifers and water tables to shrink. Almost 70% of all fresh water is used in irrigation, and about 2 billion people drink contaminated water tainted by waste and pollution. Water shortages have created more than 20,000 square miles of desert areas per year from previously arable lands. One-half of all wetlands on earth have perished in the last century. In the next two decades, about two-thirds of all of the world's population will be affected by water problems such that fresh water shortage and water quality will be the dominant problems in the next century and may potentially threaten people's health, the environment and future generations on a grand scale.

## Water Shortages

One-third of all countries on earth, which contain 40% of the world's population, are currently encountering serious water shortages, which in turn leads to lack of sanitation. In less than three decades, over 50% of the world's people could face severe difficulties in finding water for drinking and irrigation. This problem is exacerbated by the practice in developing countries of discharging wastewater without treatment into rivers and streams, which results in serious health hazards, and degradation of rivers, lakes, seas and oceans through the spread of waterborne diseases.

## Water Problems

Water problems are made more complex by a serious shortage in rainfall and debilitating drought. Although water is the most common substance on earth, 97% of the total is seawater, which is unfit for human use. Of the 3% that is fresh, two-thirds of this amount is locked up in glaciers or ice and snow around the poles. Only 1% of all the world's water is available for human consumption. The 1% of the earth's available water goes through a water cycle in which rainwater falls from the clouds onto the land, nourishes life, returns through rivers to the salty sea and evaporates as fresh water back into the clouds.

Although water is an infinitely renewable resource because of this natural cycle, three main obstacles exist in its provision to people. One obstacle is that some places have more water than they can possibly use while others have too little. In many parts of the world rainfall is highly seasonal, and almost all the year's supply may arrive within a few weeks. Since water is very heavy, it is very costly to transport it over long distances. A second obstacle with water is the extravagantly wasteful misuse of it. There is a huge cost associated with collecting, cleaning, storing and distributing it, and treating it—such as the situation with wastewater and sewage. A third obstacle with water is that where it is the scarcest—such as in the developing countries—irrigation for agriculture takes up over 90% of the available fresh water. As water consumption grows with population increases, this situation will lead to increasing water shortages—and possibly even to wars.

## The Looming Crisis

The lack of fresh water could affect two-thirds of the world's population by 2025 if governments fail to collaborate to protect and conserve it. One of the first indications of this pending water crisis will be mass migrations of people away from areas that are without water. Political tensions will follow these movements of environmental refugees as scarce water resources create a population affected by extreme water poverty. *The additional 2 billion more people that are expected in the world by 2050 will exacerbate the global crisis for a resource that does not have any substitutes.*

Mismanagement, overuse and climate change pose long-term threats to human well-being, and evaluating and responding to those threats constitutes a major challenge. Fresh water taken from rivers and ground water and deterioration through pollution will further limit the resource base, and will negatively affect the health of aquatic life forms since vegetation and wildlife are also dependent upon adequate freshwater resources. Marshes, bogs and interfaces between land and waterways are even more dependent upon sustainable water supply. But, it is forests and other ecosystems that are at greater risk of dramatic changes as water availability is diminished. Through the last 100 years, more than one-half of the Earth's wetlands have been destroyed. These wetlands are important because they are the habitats of mammals, birds, fish, amphibians, and invertebrates. They also support the growing of rice and other food crops as well as providing water filtration and protection from storms and flooding. The lack of fresh water could even limit human development.

## The Current Situation

Currently over 1.2 billion people worldwide lack access to water, and almost 3 billion people find water scarce for at least one month out of the year. Inadequate sanitation is also a problem for almost 2.5 billion people in the world. They are exposed to diseases, such as cholera and typhoid fever, and other water-borne illnesses. 2 million people die each year from diarrheal diseases, with most of them being children.

Many of the water systems that keep ecosystems thriving and feed a growing human population have become stressed. Rivers, lakes and aquifers are drying up or becoming too polluted to use. More than one-half the world's wetlands have disappeared. Agriculture consumes more water than any other source and wastes much of that through inefficiencies. At the current consumption rate, this situation will only get worse. By 2025, at the current consumption rate, two-thirds of the world's population may face water shortages, with many ecosystems around the world collapsing.

## Changes in Climate Affecting Water

Climate change is altering patterns of weather and water around the world, causing shortages and droughts in some areas and floods in others. The amount of available fresh water is decreasing because climate change has caused glaciers to recede, reduced stream and river flows, and shrunk lakes and ponds. Many aquifers have been over-pumped and much of the water obtained through them has become polluted, salted, unsuitable or otherwise unavailable for drinking, industrial and agricultural use. Because of climate change, weather patterns can be expected to change in the future. As the temperature increases through climate change, rainfall may increase in some areas, but because of evaporation these areas may get even drier.

# Unequal Distribution of Wealth

## Overview

The wealthiest nations—of which there are only a few—account for 80% of the material and energy that is consumed globally. 20% of the poorest nations account for only 1% of the total resource consumption. In these very poor nations the average wage is less than $2 per day such that the single biggest contributor to ill health and environmental destruction is poverty. This disparagement accounts for social, economic and environmental ills such as illiteracy, disease epidemics, lack of clean water, inadequate housing, destruction of forests, pollution of air, water and land, and lack of food. Also, population growth rates are the highest where the poverty levels are the most severe, and results in less security, fewer choices, less progress and a degradation in human equality, especially through unemployment. The increase in wage inequality and unavailability of jobs creates a situation of unrest and produces crime, with more prisons being built in an attempt to control the illegal activities. Eventually, this situation gives rise to extreme and violent forms of expression such as terrorism.

## The Unequal Distribution of Wealth

The distribution of wealth differs from the income distribution in that it looks at the distribution of ownership of the assets in a society, rather than the income of members of that society. The unequal distribution of wealth is the unbalanced division of wealth, assets and monetary value across a population. In the United States the top 1% are worth 70 times more than the rest of the 99%. Even within that top 1%, one-tenth of those have an average yearly income that is 540 times the national average of income in the United States, and the 160,000 wealthiest families in the United States own as much wealth as the lowest one-half of the American population.

This unequal distribution of wealth limits the amount of resources, causing a huge difference in living conditions between the haves and the have-nots. Most children have very little expectation of improving upon the condition into which they were born. This economic disadvantage for the overwhelming majority translates into ill health, missed educational opportunities, and increasing depression, alcoholism, obesity, gambling, and criminality among the dispossessed, showing that increasing wealth inequality and many other social problems are interrelated.

# Sex Exploitation and Slavery

## Overview

Slavery is illegal and is employed as a means of controlling humans to be owned, bought and sold such that they cannot withdraw from the arrangement. While a person is a slave, the owner is entitled to the productivity of the slave's labor or service, especially with regard to sex exploitation. A person may become a slave as a result of human trafficking. There are an estimated 30 million slaves worldwide who generate a multibillion-dollar industry, with estimates of up to $35 billion that is generated annually, mostly through sex activities.

## Sex Trafficking

Trafficking in human beings is the most prevalent method of obtaining slaves. Victims are recruited through deceit or trickery such as a false job offer, false migration offer, or false marriage offer, sale by family members, recruitment by former slaves, or abduction. Victims are forced into a debt slavery situation by coercion, deception, fraud, intimidation, isolation, threat, physical force, debt bondage or even force-feeding with drugs to control their victims. Approximately 80% of the victims are women and girls, and up to 50% are minors.

While the majority of trafficking victims are women and children who are forced into prostitution, victims include men who are forced into manual labor. About 800,000 people worldwide are trafficked across borders each year, and up to 2 million individuals are trafficked internally or internationally each year, with about a third of them being sex trafficking victims.

# Decimation of Forests

## Overview

An estimated 13 million hectares of forests were lost each year between 2000 and 2010 due to decimation of forests. In tropical rainforests, deforestation continues to be an urgent environmental issue that jeopardizes people's livelihoods, threatens species, and intensifies global warming. Deforestation by the clear-cutting of forest areas for uses such as agriculture and livestock grazing, urban development, mining operations and petroleum extraction has produced vast areas of wastelands. The removal of significant areas of forests has created a degraded environment with reduced biodiversity by the associated declines in habitats. It has affected and reshaped climates, and it has created a deterioration in the quality of life. In the last two centuries, the earth has undergone an unprecedented worldwide destruction of forests, with the destruction being the most pronounced in the tropical rain forests where the result has been one of mass extinctions of plant and animal species. These rain forests are being destroyed at an accelerating pace by the onslaught of rapid human population growth and associated urban development, with estimates being that 80% of existing rain forests will no longer exist by 2030—*with the prediction that all tropical forests will probably be gone by 2050.*

## The Effects of Shrinking Forests

A shrinking forest cover lessens the landscape's capacity to intercept, retain and transport precipitation, causing water runoffs directly back into the oceans. Since forests extract carbon dioxide and other pollutants from the air, their decimation affects the stability of the earth's biosphere and contributes to the enhancement of the greenhouse effect, especially by $CO_2$ through the slash-and-burn techniques of wooded areas. Trees extract groundwater through their roots and release it into the atmosphere. This natural water cycle is affected by deforestation. When a forest is removed, that region can no longer hold as much water, with the result being a much drier climate for that region. Even if large rainfall events occur, the water runoffs overwhelm the storage capacity of the remaining soil through saturation, causing severe flooding and soil erosion. The impact on the environment through deforestation is significant in that it affects the amount of water in the soil, lowers the levels of groundwater, and decreases the amount of moisture in the atmosphere.

Nearly one-half of the earth's forests are gone, and one-third of the remaining ones have been severely affected by logging. One-half of the remaining 70% of the original forests that covered the earth are currently threatened by human activities. Every year more than 100,000 square miles of forest is lost forever—as well as the plant and animal species that live in these forests. A total of one-third of all tropical forests has disappeared in the last 50 years along with thousands of plant and animal species. At the current rate of destruction, the tropical forests—which amount to 30% of the total forest area—will be gone within 30 to 50 years. With their demise, over a million species will perish—*more than what has become extinct in the last 20 million years.*

Forests are not only being cleared to make room for urban development, but are being cleared to convert the land for grazing livestock and for growing feed such as corn, oats and soybeans for consumption by the livestock. *Nearly 85% of all arable land is associated with livestock.* Some of this grazing land has been created from what were formerly virgin rain forests—environments that contain 80% of the earth's land vegetation and which provide a habitat for one-half of the earth's species.

The decimation of forests can have devastating climatic effects on the earth since the lack of trees can cause soil erosion, lead to floods because nothing is there to stop the rain runoffs, produce less oxygen for humans to breathe, and reduce the food supply by eliminating an environment in which plants can thrive. The reduction of rain forests will reduce the migratory bird populations, which in turn will increase the growth of insect pests through the loss of natural control by these birds. This forces the increase in the use of pesticides to deal with insect plagues—an effect that creates more pollution of the water and land environments.

## The Value of Forests

Forests impact our daily lives because they produce fruits, paper and wood. They generate by-products for items such as medicines, cosmetics and detergents. From the air that we breathe to the wood that we use, human beings are heavily dependent on forests and the products and services that they provide. Forests provide habitats to diverse animal species, and form the source of livelihood for many different human settlements. They offer watershed protection, timber and non-timber products, and offer recreational options. Forests prevent soil erosion, help in maintaining the water cycle, and check global warming by using carbon dioxide. When forests are taken away, it is not just the trees that go. The entire ecosystem falls apart, with dire consequences.

## The Effects of Deforestation

The effects of deforestation are many. It creates a reduced biodiversity that can cause wildlife to decline. When forest cover is removed, wildlife is deprived of habitat and becomes more vulnerable to hunting. Considering that about 80% of the world's species can be found in tropical rainforests, deforestation poses a serious threat to the Earth's biodiversity.

Deforestation can cause the release of greenhouse gas emissions. This is because forests are the largest terrestrial store of carbon, and deforestation is the third-largest source of greenhouse gas emissions after coal and oil. Deforestation causes 15% of global greenhouse gas emissions. Of these, $CO_2$ emissions represent up to one-third of the total $CO_2$ emissions that are released because of human activity.

Deforestation can disrupt water cycles and increase soil erosion. As a result of deforestation, trees can no longer evaporate groundwater, which can cause the local climate to be much drier. Deforestation accelerates the rates of soil erosion by increasing runoff and reducing the protection of the soil from tree litter. Because millions of people rely directly on forests, deforestation can create severe social problems that sometimes lead to violent conflict.

Deforestation causes forest degradation, which happens when changes within the forest negatively affect the structure or function of the stand or site, and thereby lowers the capacity to supply products and/or ecosystem services. Forest degradation creates less resilient and less productive forests and can be as harmful as deforestation. Forest degradation often begins when large canopy gaps dry out rainforests leaving them vulnerable to fire.

# Desertification

## Overview

Vast tracts of the earth are turning into dust bowls on a scale that dwarfs all previous ones. Because of this, the world may be on the verge of a greater hunger than has ever been seen in history. Tens of millions of poor people can afford to eat only five days out of the week. Most of the world is exhausting its ground water because of over-pumping. Yields are flat lining and people were running out of land to grow food. Millions of acres have been turned into wasteland because of over-farming and over-grazing. The limits of land that can be ploughed and the land available for grazing are being rapidly reached.

The removal of the topsoil makes the land too depleted to raise flocks or grow food. The abandonment of so much land, both for farming and for grazing, will restrict efforts to expand food production as the demand for food outstrips the supply. With climate change threatening the global food supply, changes in the world food system will lead to greater hardship than ever before. Low-income families have reached the point where they can no longer afford to eat everyday—not even where one meal a day is a minimum.

## The Process

Desertification creates the degradation of formerly productive in a complex process that involves multiple causes, and which has intensified as a result of human activities. Desertification can occur in areas far from natural deserts by the degradation of arable land into barren soil, rock, or sand as a result of severe droughts coupled with land abuse. More than 70% of earth's dry land is affected by desertification, which presently adversely affects approximately one billion people on earth—most of them among the poorest in the world.

Desertification results in the destruction of topsoil followed by loss of the land's ability to sustain crops, livestock or human activity. Although climatic changes can trigger the desertification process, it is human activities that are the cause, which can be as follows:

- Over-cultivation, which exhausts the soil
- Salinization, which causes the deterioration of irrigated lands
- Deforestation, which removes trees that hold the soil to the land
- Overgrazing, a process whereby livestock strips the land of grasses

Desertification also creates conditions that intensify wildfires and produce the stirring of winds. Dust from deserts is then blown into cities around the world where these dust particles are inhaled, and cause health problems—a very serious effect as the population increases.

## Causes

The major contributor of desertification is the dramatic increase in population accompanied by destructive human activities such as chopping of trees for firewood or elimination of plants that bind the soil, livestock pressures that cause erosion by overgrazing and poor practices in farming. The immediate cause of desertification is the removal of most vegetation. This is driven by a combination of drought, climatic shifts, tillage for agriculture, overgrazing and deforestation for fuel or construction materials. Vegetation plays a major role in determining the biological composition of the soil. In many environments, the rate of erosion and runoff decreases with increased vegetation cover. But, unprotected, dry soil surfaces blow away with the wind or are washed away by flash floods, leaving lower soil layers that bake in the sun and become a hardpan.

Effects on Inhabitants

About 90% of the inhabitants of dry lands live in developing nations where they suffer from poor economic and social conditions. This situation is exacerbated by land degradation because of the reduction in productivity, the precariousness of living conditions and the difficulty of access to resources and opportunities. A downward spiral is created in many underdeveloped countries by overgrazing, land exhaustion and over-drafting of groundwater in many of the marginally productive world regions. This is due to overpopulation pressures that create an exploitation of marginal dry lands for farming. When unfavorable agro-climatic conditions are combined with an absence of infrastructure and access to markets, as well as poorly adapted production techniques and an underfed and undereducated population, most of these land zones are excluded from development. Desertification causes rural lands to become unable to support the same sized populations that previously lived there. This results in mass migrations out of rural areas and into urban areas that create large numbers of unemployed people who end up living in slums or in the streets as homeless persons.

# Warfare

## Overview

Approximately 15,000 wars have been fought in the 7,000 years of existence as a civilization by human beings, with the means of destruction having become much more violent. The design of weapons is guided by a notion to inflict terrible and terrifying damage to humans and human societies—such as nuclear devices to incinerate entire cities, agents to defoliate and make uninhabitable entire country-sides, the creation of chemicals like napalm that are formulated to bind fire to human skin, and the refinement of claymore mines that are filled with metal cubes which are intended to deliver as much damage and pain as possible to human flesh and bones. As technology advances, its application to weaponry will become more lethal, have wider-ranging effects and become much more powerful to combat with conventional means.

Of the approximately 100 wars that are now being fought in the world, more than two-thirds of these originated in parts of the earth where conditions such as exhausted resources and collapsing life-support systems exist. These areas suffer from guerrillas, crime gangs, dictatorships, and a flourishing arms industry that diverts the needed money to activities that do not produce anything—except strife and death. Even in oil-producing areas there exists much conflict because of the desire to control the resources. With water becoming a very valuable resource, it appears that more conflicts are in the offing for the immediate future to control this resource.

## Terrorism

Terrorism is done with the purpose of intimidating a population or compelling a government or an international organization to do or abstain from taking action. These criminal acts are intended or calculated to provoke a state of terror in the public, with the acts meant to send a message from an illicit clandestine organization. The purpose of terrorism is to exploit the media to achieve maximum attainable publicity so as to influence the targeted audience to attain political goals.

In the new millennium, terrorism has become an increasing activity. The methods that are employed vary, but are usually acts such as bombings, shootings, stabbings and vehicular homicides. A few have utilized airplanes as guided missiles to destroy buildings and kill people in mass numbers. With the increasing weapons of war such as assault rifles becoming easily available, we can expect that these acts will be perpetrated in ever increasing acts of violence—mostly on innocent civilians.

## Increased Militarism

The ever increasing danger to the planet's inhabitants is in the alarming trend towards militarism and its associated vast assortment of weaponry. The manufacture of weapons involves levels of spending that are now measured in trillions and billions—monies that are taken away from the benefit of humankind. The resort to militarism escalates tensions and makes it easier to use force in any dispute or disagreement that might otherwise have been handled by diplomatic discussions.

The League of Nations was set up after WWI, and the United Nations was established after WWII—both as attempts to prevent another disastrous world war. Even so, there are over 250 separate sovereign nations, each of which manages its own resources, people and government according to its established culture, ethnicity and social customs. While one world government sounds ideal to combine all of these countries, the reality is that it is not feasible due to the vast diversity, different history and non-homogenous nature of people around the world. At best, a federation of nations is probably the only large-scale group that can be achieved—and this only in a limited form for global decision-making. WWIII is a distinct possibility given the amount of missiles, atom bombs and hydrogen bombs that are in existence. *Another global war may leave the planet uninhabitable for human beings.*

## Cyber Warfare
\*\*\*

Software-based intelligence may very quickly become very powerful. The reason is that it may scale in different ways from biological intelligence. Software can run faster on faster computers, parts can be distributed on more computers, different versions tested and updated on the fly and new algorithms can be incorporated that give a jump in performance. The problem is that while intelligent entities are good at achieving their goals, if the goals are badly set they can use their power to achieve disastrous ends.

One of these threats involves cyber warfare. With the advent of grid computing, security is an issue because the controls on member nodes are usually very loose. Cloud computing allows access to thousands or even millions of users in many locations. Cyber warfare can involve actions by a nation-state to penetrate another nation's computers or networks for the purposes of causing damage or disruption. It can also be used by terrorist groups, companies, political or ideological extremist groups, hackers and criminal organizations. Besides sabotage, activities can involve espionage, denial of service such as shutting down the Internet, shutting down of electrical power grids, disrupting airline control systems, or even military uses to shut down other nations' capabilities for nuclear research and weapons production.

## Nanotechnology

Nanotechnology is the control over matter with atomic or molecular precision. The problem is that with increasing power, it also increases the potential for abuses that are hard to defend against. The risk is that atomically precise manufacturing is ideal for rapid, cheap manufacturing of weapons. Any government can print large amounts of autonomous or semi-autonomous weapons, accelerating arms races that could become very fast and unstable since doing a first strike might be very tempting. Systems created by nanotechnology can be small and precise such as surveillance systems for keeping populations obedient. Through nanotechnology there might be ways of getting nuclear proliferation and climate engineering into the hands of anyone. The risk from future nanotechnology advances could be potentially disruptive.

## Robot Wars

Military robots are remote-controlled devices that are designed for military applications. Some robots, such as drones, can be used to kill soldiers and civilians. The current aim is to make robots more autonomous, eventually allowing them to operate on their own for extended periods of time. The lack of emotion, fatigue, stress and passion in robots makes them ideal killing machines. The danger is that robots could become self-sufficient and able to make their own decisions, including being able to independently choose targets to attack with weapons. Viruses and other lethal agents can be introduced into large segments of human populations through the use of robots.

# Drug Trafficking

## Overview

Drug trafficking is a black market dedicated to the cultivation, manufacture, distribution and sale of drugs that are subject to drug prohibition laws. Jurisdictions prohibit trade, except under license, of many types of drugs through the use of drug prohibition laws. The size of the global illicit drug market is estimated to be $320 billion, making it a very lucrative endeavor, which remains very difficult for authorities to thwart its widespread existence.

## Effects

The United States is adversely affected by the drug trade, The most violent regions in Central America are highly correlated with an abundance of drug trafficking activity in the United States. The illegal drug trade is directly linked to violent crimes such as murder. The effects of the illegal drug trade in the United States can be seen through its political, economic and social aspects. Increasing drug related violence was tied to the racial tension that arose during the late 20th century along with the political upheaval prevalent throughout the 1960s and 70s. The second half of the 20th century was a period when increased wealth and increased discretionary spending increased the demand for illicit drugs in the United States.

## Political Impact

A large generation, the baby boomers, came of age in the 1960s. Their social tendency to confront the law on specific issues, including illegal drugs, overwhelmed the judicial system. The government attempted to enforce the law, but with meager effect. Marijuana and cocaine became major drug products, especially across the border between the United States and Mexico.

## Social impacts

Although narcotics are illegal in the United States, they have become integrated into the nation's culture and are seen as a recreational activity by sections of the population. Illicit drugs are considered to be a commodity that has strong demand, and which are typically sold at a high value. Despite the constant effort by politicians to win the war on drugs, the United States is still the world's largest importer of illegal drugs.

With a large wave of immigrants, the United States saw an increased heterogeneity in its public. Drug related homicide and drug violence became increasingly tied to these ethnic minorities—and in the process became a common anxiety in communities across urban America. The baby boomer generation also felt the effects of the drug trade in their increased drug use. Along with substance abuse, criminal involvement, suicide and murder also increased.

## The Primary Drugs

<u>Cannabis</u>

While the recreational use of cannabis is illegal as a federal law, it is available by prescription or recommendation in 40 of the 50 states—although importation and distribution is still federally prohibited. However, the increased legalization of cannabis in the United States has led the drug cartels to smuggle less cannabis and more heroin.

<u>Alcohol</u>

Alcohol is legal in the United States even though the manufacture, sale, transportation, importation and exportation of alcoholic beverage is still subject to federal regulations. There is no drug trade with this substance as it is sold legally almost everywhere, with the only restriction being the age of the consumer. Nevertheless, alcohol addiction is a definite problem, and requires the availability of alcoholic rehabilitation centers

<u>Heroin</u>

The majority of the world's heroin used to be produced in an area known as the Golden Triangle where the borders of Thailand, Laos, and Myanmar meet. However, now almost 93% of the opiates originate from Afghanistan, with an export value of $64 billion. Another significant area where poppy fields are grown for the manufacture of heroin is Mexico. According to the DEA the price of heroin is typically 10 times that of cocaine on American streets, making it a high-profit substance for smugglers and dealers.

Although it has become more difficult for drugs to be imported into the United States, that does not stop the heroin smugglers from getting their product across United States borders. A security wall that is being built along the border between Mexico and the United States may stem the flow of immigrants, but it will not curtail the drug smugglers who can use circulating saws to cut through it, who can easily scale the wall with ladders, who can tunnel under it, and who can use drones to fly over the wall with the drugs.

In Afghanistan, the war was supposed to stem the flow of opiates, but a decision was made not to interfere with the drug growing so as not to economically impact farmers who earn about a quarter of the profits, with the rest going to district officials, insurgents, warlords and drug traffickers in a country that is overrun by corruption and violence.

<u>Methamphetamine</u>

Methamphetamine is a very popular drug among distributors, with a great number of clandestine labs making the product. There are also rolling math labs, which can be concealed on large vehicles, or transported on a motorcycle. These labs are very difficult to detect, and can often be obscured among legal cargo in big trucks. Methamphetamine is sometimes used intravenously, placing users and their partners at risk for transmission of HIV and hepatitis C. Methamphetamine can also be inhaled, and is most commonly vaporized on aluminum foil or in a glass pipe to give a brief, but intense high.

Temazepam

Temazepam is a strong hypnotic benzodiazepine, which is illicitly manufactured in clandestine laboratories. Temazepam, ranks among the top illegal drugs that are most frequently abused. Temazepam affects chemicals in the brain that may be unbalanced in people with sleep problems and cause insomnia. It can also cause birth defects or life-threatening withdrawal symptoms in a newborn.

Temazepam is habit-forming and can cause severe problems, especially for someone who has a history of drug abuse or addiction. Its misuse can cause addiction, overdose, or death. It can also severely impact people who have asthma, who suffer from COPD, who are afflicted with kidney or liver disease, or who have a history of depression or suicidal thoughts or behavior. Even in its lesser effects, temazepam may cause severe allergic reactions, such as hives, difficulty in breathing, and swelling of the face, lips, tongue, or throat. Some people who used temazepam have engaged in driving, and later have no memory of doing so. Temazepam can even pass into breast milk and may harm a nursing baby.

Cocaine

Cocaine is a highly prominent drug among many drug dealers and manufacturers. The cocaine black market distribution industry is worth more than $85 billion. It has been massively produced by notorious drug dealers of cartel organizations.

Cocaine is a strong stimulant that is most frequently used as a recreational drug. It is commonly snorted, inhaled as smoke, or dissolved and injected into a vein. Mental effects include loss of contact with reality, an intense feeling of happiness, or agitation. Physical symptoms may include a fast heart rate, sweating, and large pupils.

Cocaine acts by inhibiting the reuptake of serotonin, norepinephrine, and dopamine in the brain This results in greater concentrations of these three neurotransmitters in the brain, which can then easily cross the blood–brain barrier and may lead to the breakdown of the barrier. Following repeated doses, a person may have decreased ability to feel pleasure, and be very physically tired.

Cocaine is addictive due to its effect on the reward pathway in the brain. After a short period of use, dependence will occur. Its use also increases the risk of stroke, myocardial infarction, lung problems in those who smoke it, blood infections, and sudden cardiac death. Cocaine sold on the street is commonly mixed with local anesthetics, cornstarch, quinine or sugar, which can result in additional toxicity. With further processing, crack cocaine can be produced from cocaine. It is estimated that the illegal market for cocaine in the United States is $500 billion each year. Cocaine causes over 4,000 deaths per year.

Opioids

Opioids are a homegrown problem in the United States in which addictive opioid drugs have become overused and misused with significant medical, social and economic consequences, including overdose deaths, which annually kills over 50,000 people in the United States. Opioids are strong painkillers, and include drugs such as OxyContin, Percocet, Vicodin, Norco and fentanyl. The potency and availability of these substances, despite their high risk of addiction and overdose, have made them popular both as medical treatments and as recreational drugs. Due to their sedative effects on the part of the brain which regulates breathing, opioids in high doses present the potential for respiratory depression and may cause respiratory failure and death. Although opioids are effective for treating acute pain, they are less useful for treating chronic pain, especially since the risks often outweigh the benefits.

The opioid crisis began with over-prescription of opioids in the 1990s, which led to them becoming the most prescribed class of medications in the United States. Opioids initiated for post-surgery or pain management are one of the leading causes of opioid misuse. When people continue to use opioids beyond what a doctor prescribes, it can lead to opiate addiction, with a tolerance developing and eventually leading to dependence, especially when a person relies on the drug to prevent withdrawal symptoms.

Around 100 million people or a third of the United States population is estimated to be affected by chronic pain. This has led to a push by drug companies and the federal government to expand the use of painkilling opioids. In turn, this has exacerbated the already increasing number of opioids that are being prescribed by doctors to patients, with over 300 million prescriptions being written for opioid drugs per year. Also, the structure of the United States healthcare system, in which people not qualifying for government programs are required to obtain private insurance, favors prescribing drugs over more expensive therapies.

## Is There Any Solution?

Curtailing the inflow of drugs into the United States will not stop the drug epidemic. Throwing more money at it will not stop people from using drugs. Educating the young only goes so far since as they grow into adulthood, they are swayed by peers and self-indulgence to try drugs. In fact, most experimentation with illicit drug use begins during adolescence. And, youngsters who become involved with drugs beyond experimental use are at greater risk of failing to accomplish necessary educational and developmental tasks. So what can be done? The use of illegal drugs has been a long-standing problem in American society, and is a problem that has taken on a particular urgency in the last three decades. Drug abuse is a serious and many-faceted problem. Premature mortality, epidemiologic consequences, and economic costs of illness associated with drug use are affecting all sectors of society. It all comes down to awareness: the realization that drug use will impair the brain—the valuable and irreplaceable organ of perception, insight, observation, problem-solving and intelligence.

# Weapon Development

# Biological Weapons

## Overview

Offensive biological warfare (BW) was outlawed by the 1972 Biological Weapons Convention that. has been ratified or acceded to by 170 countries. The purpose was to prevent a biological attack, which could conceivably result in large numbers of civilian casualties and cause severe disruption to economic and societal infrastructure. However, many countries currently pursue research into the defense or protection against BW.

A nation or group that can pose a credible threat of mass casualty has the ability to alter the terms on which other nations or groups interact with it. Biological weapons allow for the potential to create a level of destruction and loss of life far in excess of nuclear, chemical or conventional weapons, relative to their mass and cost of development and storage. Biological agents may be useful as strategic deterrents in addition to their utility as offensive weapons on the battlefield.

As a tactical weapon for military use, a significant problem with a BW attack is that it would take days to be effective, and therefore might not immediately stop an opposing force. Some biological agents have the capability of person-to-person transmission via aerosolized respiratory droplets. This feature can be undesirable, as the agents may be transmitted by this mechanism to unintended populations, including neutral or even friendly forces. While containment of BW is less of a concern for certain criminal or terrorist organizations, it remains a significant concern for the military and civilian populations of all nations. The use of biological weapons is prohibited under customary international humanitarian law as well as by a variety of international treaties. The use of biological agents in armed conflict is a war crime.

## The Aspects of Biological Warfare

Biological weapons, or germ warfare, are living organisms or replicating entities that reproduce or replicate within their host victims. Germ warfare is the use of biological toxins or infectious agents such as bacteria, viruses, and fungi with the intent to kill or incapacitate humans, animals or plants as an act of war. Diseases that are considered or known to be used as biological weapons include anthrax, Ebola, black plague, cholera, typhus, yellow fever and smallpox.

Biological weapons may be employed in various ways to gain an advantage over the enemy, either by threats or by actual deployments. Biological weapons may also be useful as area denial weapons. These lethal agents can be targeted against an entire population. They may be developed, acquired, stockpiled or deployed by nation states or by terrorist groups.

It is now possible to make diseases even nastier through biotechnology. As biotechnology becomes more advanced, more groups will be able to make diseases worse. Most work on bioweapons has been done by governments looking for something controllable, because wiping out humanity is not militarily useful. But there are always some people who might want to do things regardless of the consequences such as creating an apocalypse by using bioweapons. As technology gets more powerful in the future nastier pathogens will become easier to design, and the number of fatalities from such a bioweapon would become very high.

But perhaps the greatest threat to humanity from biological sources is the deliberate intention to create horrible and devastating biological weapons. These rely on agents such as smallpox, anthrax, West Nile virus and other human-mutated strains that can be delivered to populations in times of war. Entomological (insect) warfare is also considered a type of biological weapon.

## Terrorism Threats

Biological weapons are difficult to detect, economical and easy to use, making them appeal to terrorists. Their production is very easy as common technology can be used to produce biological warfare, like that used in production of vaccines, foods, spray devices, beverages and antibiotics. A major factor about biological warfare that attracts terrorists is that they can easily escape before the government agencies or secret agencies have even started their investigation. This is because the potential organism has incubation period of 3 to 7 days, after which the results begin to appear, and thereby giving terrorists a lead time to escape.

Ricin, other toxins and cyanide attacks have also been used by terrorists. A lone terrorist having adequate knowledge of company biological plants can cause potential danger by injecting a deadly or harmful substance into the plant. Biological weapons can also target fisheries as well as water-based vegetation. Diseases such as wheat blast and rice blast can be weaponized in aerial spray tanks and cluster bombs for delivery to enemy watersheds in agricultural regions to initiate epidemics among plants. Other weapons include foot-and-mouth disease for livestock, rinderpest to be used against cows, African swine fever to kill pigs, and psittacosis to kill chickens.

## Entomological Warfare

Entomological warfare (EW) uses insects to attack the enemy. EW has been used in battle by Japan and several other nations have developed and been accused of using an entomological warfare program. EW may employ insects in a direct attack or as vectors to deliver a biological agent such as plague. EW exists in three varieties. One type of EW involves infecting insects with a pathogen and then dispersing the insects over target areas. The insects then infect any person or animal that they might bite. A second type of EW is a direct insect attack against crops The insect may not be infected with any pathogen, but is a threat to agriculture. The third type uses uninfected insects, such as bees, wasps, etc., to directly attack the enemy.

## Modern Developments

Supposedly, rational state actors would never use biological weapons offensively because biological weapons cannot be controlled, and the weapon could backfire and harm its own army. An agent like smallpox or other airborne viruses would almost certainly spread worldwide and ultimately infect the user's home country. However, this argument does not necessarily apply to bacteria. Anthrax can easily be controlled and created in a garden shed. Using microbial methods, bacteria can be modified to be effective in only a narrow environmental range. Such a weapon may be used to bog down an advancing army, making them more vulnerable to counterattack.

A new technique in which a DNA sequence is cut off and replaced with a new sequence could potentially create a new organism. This technique represents a potential danger if used by people with wrong intentions by using genome editing technology.

Genetic warfare approaches in biotechnology, such as synthetic biology could be used in the future to design novel types of biological warfare agents. These could render a vaccine to be ineffective, they could confer resistance to antibiotics, would enhance the virulence, host range and transmissibility of a pathogen, and would enable the evasion of diagnostic or detection tools.

# Chemical Weapons

## Overview

Chemical warfare (*CW*) involves using the toxic properties of chemical substances as weapons. This type of warfare depends upon the unique properties of the chemical agent that is weaponized. A lethal chemical agent is designed to injure, incapacitate, or kill an opposing force, or to deny unhindered use of a particular area of terrain. Defoliants are used to quickly kill vegetation and deny its use for cover and concealment. CW can be used against agriculture and livestock to promote hunger and starvation. Chemical payloads can be delivered by remote controlled container release by aircraft, rocket or drone. The most common methods of dispersion of chemical agents are by munitions, bombs, projectiles, spray tanks and warheads.

## Aspects of Chemical Warfare

Many nations possess vast stockpile of weaponized agents in preparation for wartime use. About 70 different chemicals have been used or stockpiled as chemical warfare agents during the 20th century. Some of these include nerve agents, phosgene gas, mustard gas and chlorine gas as well as blister agents, nerve agents, blood agents, choking agents, tear gas, pepper spray. Such agents are acid-forming compounds that attack open skin, eyes and the respiratory system, resulting in burns and respiratory problems as a minimum effect and serious injury, blindness, temporary incapacitation or death as a maximum effect. Some chemical agents are designed to produce mind-altering changes that render the victim unable to perform their assigned mission.

# Radiological Weapons

## Overview

Radiological warfare is any form of warfare involving deliberate radiation poisoning or contamination of an area with radiological sources. A low-tech radiological weapon such as a "dirty bomb" or radiological dispersal device, refers to a conventional explosive bomb with a radiological side effect due to strapping radiation sources to it. It is a very inefficient way to spread radiation, and all such weapons have problems that render them impractical for military uses.

However, radiological warfare with dirty bombs would be of use to terrorists who are intent on spreading or intensifying fear, uncertainty and doubt. The release of radioactive material may involve no special weapon, and include no direct killing of people from its radiation source, but rather could make whole areas or structures unusable for the support of human life. The elevated radiation levels in the targeted areas would make these areas dangerous to humans. An area, once contaminated with radiation, is often expensive to clean up, and the decontamination of the affected environment would also take time.

# Nuclear Weapons

## Overview

A nuclear weapon derives its destructive force from a combination of fission and fusion reactions. Both bomb types release large quantities of energy from relatively small amounts of matter. A nuclear device no larger than traditional bombs can devastate an entire city by blast, fire, and radiation. Nuclear weapons have been used twice in war, both times by the United States against Japan. These bombings caused injuries that resulted in the instantaneous deaths of approximately 120,000 civilians and military personnel—and many thousands more since then due to secondary effects. Since the time that these two bombs were detonated, over 2,000 nuclear bombs have been tested by various countries, with the modernization of weapons continuing to this day.

## Nuclear Fission Weapons

All existing nuclear weapons derive some of their explosive energy from nuclear fission reactions. Weapons whose explosive output is exclusively from fission reactions are atomic bombs. In fission weapons, a mass of enriched uranium or plutonium is forced into super criticality—allowing an exponential growth of nuclear chain reactions. All fission reactions generate products that are radioactive, and are the principal radioactive component of nuclear fallout.

## Nuclear Fusion Weapons

Nuclear fusion weapons are hydrogen bombs that rely on fusion reactions between deuterium and tritium. When a fission bomb is detonated, gamma rays and X-rays are emitted and react to create enormous numbers of high-speed neutrons, which trigger the explosion and leave behind depleted uranium. The largest nuclear weapon ever detonated was by the USSR, which released an energy equivalent of over 50 megatons of TNT. Fusion reactions do not create fission products, and contribute less nuclear fallout than fission reactions, but because all thermonuclear weapons contain at least one fission stage, these weapons can generate at least as much nuclear fallout as fission-only weapons.

## Boosted Fission Weapon

A boosted fission weapon is a fission bomb that increases its explosive yield through a small number of fusion reactions, but it is not a fusion bomb. In the boosted bomb, the neutrons produced by the fusion reactions serve primarily to increase the efficiency of the fission bomb.

## Neutron Bomb

A neutron bomb is a thermonuclear weapon that yields a relatively small explosion but a relatively large amount of neutron radiation. Such a device could be used to cause massive casualties while leaving infrastructure mostly intact and creating a minimal amount of fallout. Damage from a neutron bomb is focused on biological life rather than on material infrastructure although extreme blast and heat effects are not eliminated. Most of the injuries caused by a neutron bomb come from ionizing radiation, and not from heat and blast.

## Cobalt Bomb

A cobalt bomb is a nuclear weapon that would be capable of destroying all life on Earth by producing deadly fallout by releasing penetrating gamma radiation. The lethal fallout would have a half-life of 5¼ years and would be intensely radioactive. The airborne particles would settle and coat the earth's surface before any significant decay has occurred, thus making it impractical to hide in shelters. However, the mass needed to cover the earth's surface would be very large, and the fallout would not reach all areas in equal proportions and would disperse unevenly due to forces such as winds. There is no maximum size limit for a bomb of this type.

## Salted Bomb

Surrounding a nuclear weapon with materials such as zinc, tantalum or gold creates a weapon known as a salted bomb, which is a device that can produce exceptionally large quantities of long-lived radioactive contamination. Such a device could serve as a "doomsday weapon" because such a large quantity of radioactivity with half-lives of decades would be lifted into the stratosphere where winds would distribute it around the globe, and would make all life on the planet extinct.

## Pure Fusion Bomb

Research has been done into the possibility of pure fusion bombs, which are nuclear weapons that consist of fusion reactions without requiring a fission bomb to initiate them. Pure fusion weapons would create significantly less nuclear fallout because they would not disperse fission products.

## Antimatter Bombs

Antimatter, which consists of particles resembling having opposite electric charge, has been considered as a trigger mechanism for nuclear weapons. A major obstacle is the difficulty of producing antimatter in large enough quantities. It may also be theoretically possible to make one as the explosive itself.

**Apocalyptic Scenarios**

# Decreasing Biodiversity

## Species Extinction

The current rate of species extinction—a process that has occurred in the last 50 years—is about *one hundred per day*. At this rate, earth will lose one-half of all species in the next 50 years. Hunting, pollution and climate change have contributed towards the mass extinction process, and all of these have been influenced by human activities. It is an unprecedented event that is leading to the loss of potential medicines, pristine habitats and wildlife. The decrease in biological diversity affects everything—especially humans—and it may lead to the possible extinction of humanity itself.

In recent times, the activities of humanity have resulted in an unprecedented assault on all life forms. The decreases in biodiversity are due to killing by weapons, instruments, pesticides, pollution from toxic chemicals and global warming. But, the most pervasive form of species destruction has come from habitat destruction, which is due to factors such as the expansion of agricultural land use, increasing timber production, more mining, increased industrial development, and continual growth in transportation with its many roads, airports, canals and railroads. These have caused local ecosystems to undergo major changes, with many species not being unable to adapt, and perishing as a result.

## Species Depletion

Humanity has destroyed 75% of the world's crop plant species since 1900. Human-caused species extinction has accelerated from 1,000 species per year in 1970 to more than 10,000 species per year since 2000. At this rate, almost 33% of all current life forms will be extinct within 20 years. Many of the remaining species will be in an endangered state as the most diverse ecosystem on earth—the tropical rain forests—are destroyed at an alarming rate by an encroaching human population. Coral reefs, which are a haven for many species of plants and animals, are the second most diverse ecosystem on earth, and are referred to as the "rainforests of the sea". With the destruction of coral reefs, many organisms have lost their habitat forever, resulting in a decrease in the number of plants and animals in the oceans. Another damaging effect is the creation of "dead zones" in the oceans where marine life can no longer exist due to the depletion of oxygen from the water caused by garbage and the accumulation of plastic.

## The Impact

The main concern with decreasing biodiversity is that all organisms are interrelated, and they play a vital role in maintaining the cycle of life. The usefulness of various plant and animal species in the production of food and medicines makes the preservation of biodiversity very important for human well-being. Human survival is dependent on the natural world remaining intact in a sustainable manner. The greater the loss of animal and plant life becomes, the more serious the consequences will be for mankind. Without some critical species being around—such as the honeybee—we may even perish.

# Bees, Bats and Amphibians

Three Major Concerns

Through a phenomenon termed as "colony collapse disorder" billions of honeybees have disappeared since 2006—they have simply just vanished from their hives. In turn, this has affected 33% of the flowering food crops such as fruits, vegetables and nuts—as well as the production of honey. It is a phenomenon with a wide-reaching impact in that *all* flowering plants—including animal-feed crops such as clover that is fed to dairy cows and alfalfa, which is fed to livestock—require pollination and need honeybees to survive. *If present rates of annihilation continue, the expectation is that all honeybees will cease to exist by 2035.* This is a critical situation since of the 100 crop species responsible for providing 90% of the food worldwide, 71 of these are dependent on bee pollination. This constitutes a direct threat to the food supply since if honeybee extinction were to occur, humanity would be relegated to a diet consisting mainly of rice, corn and wheat.

The bat population is going through a traumatic change. Hundreds of thousands of bats are dying from a fungus disorder called "white nose syndrome" that affects their noses, and causes them to expend extra energy because of lack of sleep. The bats deplete their fat stores and go out to search for additional food, with many of them dying in winter when they are supposed to be hibernating. Since each bat eats about 1,000 insects daily, their depletion bodes dire consequences for humans if the insect population suddenly increases and devastates the crops. Bats pollinate plants and keep in check the populations of mosquitoes, which carry diseases that affect humans. The absence of bats will have grave consequences for humanity.

The amphibians are experiencing a current threat extinction of approximately one-third of the 6,300 known world's species. Over one-half of these species are estimated to be extinct by 2050. These amphibian life forms include salamanders, frogs, toads, lizards, chameleons, caecilians and snakes, and they represent "the canaries in the coal mine" for humanity. A new fungus disease that kills frogs and toads and every other species of amphibian is spreading around the globe and—which combined with pollution and overdevelopment—is driving more of the amphibians to extinction. If the amphibians become extinct—and they are not doing very well at present—*then humanity is next on the list to become extinct.*

# Worldwide Pandemic

## Overview

A pandemic is an epidemic of disease that has spread across a large region, across multiple continents, or even worldwide. This is different from a widespread endemic disease that is stable in terms of how many people are getting sick from it. Flu pandemics generally exclude recurrences of seasonal flu. Throughout history, there have been a number of pandemics, such as smallpox and tuberculosis. One of the most devastating pandemics was the Black Death, which killed 100 million people in the 14th century. The most recent pandemic is the HIV virus, which started in Africa and that has claimed 32 million deaths while infecting 44 million people who are still living. Another pandemic was the 1918 Spanish Flu, which infected 500 million people and killed 50 million people. There is also the 2009 H1N1 pandemic, which killed 575,000 people. Currently, there is a Wuhan coronavirus, which started in China and that is spreading across the entire globe.

## The Effects of a Pandemic

A pandemic affects a large number of people, and can also occur in agricultural organisms such as livestock, crop plants, fish, tree species or birds. There is a six-stage classification process by which a novel virus moves from the first few infections in humans to a pandemic. This starts with the virus mostly infecting animals, with a few cases where animals infect people, and then moves through the stage where the virus begins to spread directly between people. It ends when infections from the virus have spread worldwide. Unless something is done, a pandemic will be out of control and will end in a global outbreak.

## History

There have been plagues beginning with the Plague of Athens, which started in 430 BCE. The Black Death plague started in 1331 and killed 100 million people. A plague pandemic that started in China in 1855 and which spread to India killed 10 million people. In the 19th century, cholera killed tens of millions of people. The Spanish flu of 1918 that was prevalent during WWI infected and killed 50 million people. In the mid-1950s, the Asian flu caused 2 million deaths. In the late 1960s, the Hong Kong flu killed one million people. During the 20th century, smallpox was responsible for 500 million deaths. In the last 150 years, measles has killed 200 million people. Tuberculosis affects 8 million people yearly and causes 2 million deaths, and during the 20th century has killed 100 million people. Malaria affects 500 million people each year.

## Possible Future Pandemics

Viral hemorrhagic fevers, such as the Ebola virus, are highly contagious and deadly diseases, with the potential to become pandemics. Antibiotic-resistant microorganisms (superbugs) may contribute to the re-emergence of diseases which are currently well controlled. SARS is a dangerously contagious disease that is caused by a coronavirus, which originated from bats. The Middle East respiratory syndrome MERS is a viral respiratory infection caused by a coronavirus, which was also derived from bats. The Zika virus, which began in 2015 has caused 1,5 million people to become infected, and is transmitted by mosquitoes. Currently, the Wuhan coronavirus, which originated from snakes, has affected thousands, killed hundreds, and has spread worldwide.

Aside from the economic consequences of pandemic events, the real danger is the evolution of a virus that is incurable. If such a virus spreads, then the effect will be to wipe out most of humanity, assuming that a few individuals miraculously develop an immunity. If such a situation prevails, then civilization as we know it will forever be lost, and the few remaining people will be left in a post-apocalyptic world.

# Nuclear Holocaust

## Overview

A nuclear holocaust involves widespread destruction and radioactive fallout causing the collapse of civilization through the use of nuclear weapons. Under such a scenario, some or all of the Earth will be made uninhabitable. Besides the immediate destruction of cities by nuclear blasts, the potential aftermath of a nuclear war could involve firestorms, a nuclear winter, a nuclear spring, widespread radiation sickness from the fallout, and the loss of modern electronic technology devices due to electromagnetic pulses. A thermonuclear war could result in the end of modern civilization on earth.

Billions of humans would survive the immediate effects of nuclear blasts and radiation following a global thermonuclear war. But, a nuclear war could indirectly contribute to human extinction via the secondary effects, including environmental consequences, social breakdown and economic collapse. Even a relatively small-scale nuclear exchange, such as a nuclear war between India and Pakistan could cause a nuclear winter and kill more than a billion people.

## The Doomsday Clock

The "Doomsday Clock" of the *Bulletin of the Atomic Scientists* has visualized how close the world is to a nuclear war. The Doomsday Clock is a symbol which represents the likelihood of a man-made global catastrophe. The symbol has been maintained since 1947 by the members of the *Bulletin of the Atomic Scientists*. The Doomsday Clock is a metaphor for threats to humanity from unchecked scientific and technical advances, and represents the hypothetical global catastrophe as "midnight" and the *Bulletin*'s opinion on how close the world is to a global catastrophe as the number of "minutes" to midnight. The factors influencing the Doomsday Clock are nuclear risk and climate change. Currently, it is set at 100 seconds to midnight—the closest that it has ever been.

## The Likelihood of a Nuclear War

Currently, there are 15,000 nuclear weapons possessed by a few countries. thousands of which are on hair-trigger alert. While stockpiles have been on the decline, every nuclear country is undergoing modernization of its nuclear arsenal. This modernization may increase the risk of nuclear proliferation, nuclear terrorism, and accidental nuclear war. The probability of complete human extinction by nuclear weapons is 1%, the probability of 1 billion dead is 10%, and the probability of 1 million dead is 30%. Even a small-scale nuclear war between two countries could have devastating global consequences, and such local conflicts are more likely than a full-scale nuclear war.

## The Likelihood of Complete Human Extinction

A global thermonuclear war with the nuclear stockpiles that are currently available may lead to human extinction. Although total extinction may not happen, parts of the world would remain uninhabitable. While the risk may not be zero, the climactic effects of nuclear war are uncertain and could be larger. There could also be indirect risks, such as a societal collapse following nuclear war that can make humanity much more vulnerable to other existential threats.

If a future nuclear arms race someday leads to larger stockpiles or more dangerous nuclear weapons than existed before, at what point could a war with such weapons result in human extinction? Also, a deliberate "doomsday device" could be constructed by surrounding powerful hydrogen bombs with a massive amount of cobalt. Cobalt has a half-life of 5 years, and its global fallout might be able to clear out all human life through lethal radiation intensity. A cobalt bomb, which is a doomsday device, does not need to be launched before detonation, and does not require expensive missile delivery systems. The atomic and hydrogen bombs do not need to be miniaturized for delivery by missiles. The nuclear bombs could also be laced with aerosols designed to exacerbate nuclear winter.

## The Effects of Nuclear War

It is difficult to estimate the total number of deaths resulting from a global nuclear exchange because new effects of nuclear weapons are being discovered. Early reports considered direct effects from nuclear blast and radiation and indirect effects from economic, social, and political disruption. A 1979 report for the Senate by the Office of Technology Assessment estimated casualties under different scenarios. For a full-scale nuclear exchange between the United States and the Soviet Union, they predicted United States deaths would be from 70 million to 160 million, and that Soviet deaths would range from 20% to 40% of their population. Although this report was made when nuclear stockpiles were at much higher levels than they are today, it was made before the risk of nuclear winter was first theorized in the early 1980s. It also did not consider other secondary effects, such as electromagnetic pulses and the ramifications they would have on modern technology and industry.

### Nuclear Winter

In the early 1980s, scientists began to consider the effects of smoke and soot arising from burning wood, plastics, and petroleum fuels in nuclear-devastated cities. It was speculated that the intense heat would carry these particulates to extremely high altitudes where they could drift for weeks and block out all but a fraction of the sun's light. A 1983 study was the first to model these effects, which coined the term "nuclear winter". More recent studies have made use of global circulation models and computer power to examine the consequences of a global nuclear war involving large portions of the current global nuclear arsenal. The study found that cooling in the core farming regions of the United States, Europe, Russia and China would occur for the first two summer growing seasons. Soot in the upper stratosphere, where precipitation does not occur, would last for 10 years. Global cooling would also cause a weakening of the global hydrological cycle, reducing global precipitation by 50%. No food production for a year would mean that most of the people on the planet would run out of food and starve to death.

Even small-scale, regional nuclear conflicts could disrupt the global climate for a decade or more. If as much as five million tons of soot are released, this would produce a cooling of several degrees over large areas of North American and Eurasia, including most of the grain-growing regions. The cooling would last for years, and would be catastrophic due to failure of the monsoons.

Regional nuclear conflicts could also inflict significant damage to the ozone layer. A 2008 study found that a regional nuclear weapons exchange could create a near-global ozone hole, triggering human health problems and impacting agriculture for at least a decade. This effect on the ozone layer would result from heat absorption by soot in the upper stratosphere, which would modify wind currents and draw in ozone-destroying nitrogen oxides. These high temperatures and nitrogen oxides would reduce the ozone layer to the same dangerous levels that are now experienced below the ozone hole above Antarctica every year.

Nuclear Famine

It is difficult to estimate the number of casualties that would result from a nuclear winter, but it is likely that the primary effect would be global famine in which mass starvation would occur due to disrupted agricultural production and distribution. More than 2 billion people would be at risk of starvation in the event of a regional nuclear exchange, such as between India and Pakistan, or by the use of even a small proportion of nuclear arms held by the United States and Russia. Several agricultural outputs would be significantly reduced for years by climatic changes driven by nuclear wars. Reduction of food supply would be further exacerbated by rising food prices, affecting hundreds of millions of vulnerable people, especially in the poorest nations of the world.

Electromagnetic Pulse

An electromagnetic pulse (EMP) is a burst of electromagnetic radiation. Nuclear explosions create EMP that interferes by disrupting or damaging electronic equipment. If a single nuclear weapon designed to emit EMP were detonated 250 to 300 miles up over the middle of the United States, it would disable the electronics in the entire country.

Given that many of the comforts and necessities that we enjoy are predicated on electronics and their functioning, an EMP would disable hospitals, water treatment facilities, food storage facilities, and all electronic forms of communication. An EMP blast would threaten the foundation which supports the existence of the modern human condition. Certain EMP attacks could lead to a large loss of power for months or even years. Currently, failures of the power grid are dealt with by using support from the outside. In the event of an EMP attack, such support would not exist and all damaged components, devices, and electronics would need to be completely replaced.

The problem of protecting civilian infrastructure from electromagnetic pulse has been intensively studied. A nuclear EMP is the most significant threat to the United States. The greatest threat to human survival in the aftermath of an EMP blast would be the inability to access clean drinking water. Other countries would similarly see the resurgence of previously non-existent diseases as clean water became increasingly scarce.

Nuclear Fallout

Nuclear fallout is the residual radioactive dust and ash propelled into the upper atmosphere following a nuclear explosion. Nuclear fallout is usually limited to the immediate area, and can only spread for hundreds of miles from the explosion site if the explosion is high enough in the atmosphere. Fallout may get mixed with clouds and fall as black rain.

The radioactive dust, usually consisting of fission products mixed with bystanding atoms that are neutron activated by exposure, is a highly dangerous kind of radioactive contamination. The main radiation hazard from nuclear fallout is due to short-lived radionuclides external to the body. While most of the particles carried by nuclear fallout decay rapidly, some radioactive particles will have half-lives of seconds to a few months. Some radioactive isotopes are very long lived and will create radioactive hot spots for up to 5 years after the nuclear explosion. Fallout and black rain may contaminate waterways, agriculture, and soil. Contact with radioactive materials can lead to radiation poisoning through external exposure or accidental consumption. In acute doses over a short amount of time radiation will lead to prodromal syndrome, bone marrow death, central nervous system death and gastrointestinal death. Over longer periods of exposure to radiation, cancer becomes the main health risk. Long term radiation exposure can also lead to in utero effects on human development and transgenerational genetic damage.

# Runaway Greenhouse

A runaway greenhouse effect is when there is enough of a greenhouse gas in a planet's atmosphere such that the gas blocks thermal radiation from the planet, preventing the planet from cooling and from having liquid water on its surface. The runaway greenhouse effect, which is due to higher surface temperatures, means that the planet cannot cool down, and will continue to heat up. If water vapor that is produced by the high temperatures reaches the stratosphere and escapes into space, the result is a desiccated planet.

Early investigations on the effect of atmospheric carbon dioxide levels on the runaway greenhouse limit found that it would take orders of magnitude of higher amounts of $CO_2$ to take the Earth to a runaway greenhouse state. This is because $CO_2$ is not anywhere near as effective at blocking outgoing radiation as water is. Within current models of the runaway greenhouse effect, $CO_2$ does not seem capable of providing the necessary insulation for the Earth to reach the runaway effect.

However, it may be possible for $CO_2$ to push surface temperatures such that runaway greenhouse conditions can occur on the Earth, especially by burning coal and mining oil sands. A re-evaluation of the effect of water vapor in the climate models showed that this outcome might be possible, but requires ten times the amount of $CO_2$ we could release from burning all the oil, coal, and natural gas in the Earth's crust. But, the uncertainty in whether greenhouse gases can create a greenhouse effect is due to how much $CO_2$, methane, nitrous oxide and other gases will be produced in the future.

The concentration of $CO_2$ in Earth's atmosphere has already reached a record high in 2019. The global average concentrations of the greenhouse gas, which is a byproduct of burning fossil fuels, reached 415 parts per million. This follows a trend that shows that the planet is continuing to warm at an alarming pace. There is no sign of a slowdown, or decline, in greenhouse gases concentration in the atmosphere despite all of the commitments that were made by the countries of the world under the Paris Agreement on Climate Change.

$CO_2$ traps heat from the sun and can linger in the atmosphere for centuries. High levels of the greenhouse gas are associated with higher global temperatures and other effects of climate change, such as melting polar ice caps and rising sea levels. The level of carbon dioxide in the atmosphere has risen sharply as a result of human activities, with the current global average representing a 147% increase over the pre-industrial level. The last time that the Earth experienced a comparable concentration of $CO_2$ was 5 million years ago. The concern is that countries have failed to halt the rise of greenhouse gas emissions—despite repeated warnings from scientists. China and the United States, the world's biggest polluters, have continued to expand their carbon footprints.

The concentrations of two other greenhouse gases, methane and nitrous oxide, have also seen an uptick over the past decade. Methane is an especially potent greenhouse gas and global average concentrations of methane have reached 1,869 parts per billion, a 259% increase over pre-industrial levels. It is estimated that about 60% of methane emissions come from human activities, such as from landfills, cattle breeding and certain types of agriculture, while the other 40% comes from natural sources. Nitrous oxide, which is emitted from agricultural and industrial activities, is the third-most potent greenhouse gas and depletes the ozone layer that shields the planet from the sun's ultraviolet radiation. Atmospheric concentrations of nitrous oxide have reached an average of 331.1 parts per billion, which is a 123% increase over pre-industrial levels.

A runaway greenhouse effect might still happen if enough greenhouse gases are produced, potentially spelling the end of all life on Earth. As the surface temperature of Earth reaches 117 °F or more, the temperature of Earth will then rise rapidly and its oceans will boil away until it becomes intolerably hot. As the water escapes, the Earth will cease in its life sustaining capabilities.

# The Future of America

For over 250 years of its existence, the country has been involved in wars—except for only 16 of those years. The United States is currently spending billions on war and defense instead of investing in the infrastructure and the environment, and in new technologies that will produce new industries and create jobs for the population. The critical point in the nation has been reached where it is very important to do things that help our population survive and thrive. In doing so we will also help the rest of the world, especially if they model us in pursuing the same goals. Wasting more money on weapons of mass destruction is a pointless exercise since we already have enough weapons to destroy the entire human race. But, defense spending can still be done at a reasonable level to develop new technologies and systems for ships, tanks, aircraft, submarines, missiles, drones, sonar, radar and laser weapons.

Investing in the United States economy will boost the economy, make the country stronger, reduce unemployment by creating jobs, and will revitalize key industries and create new manufacturing companies. There is a great potential for the United States to launch new projects. In contrast to the $7 trillion that has been spent on the wars in Iraq and Afghanistan, the investment in the infrastructure of the nation would require about 1% of this amount. We have gotten very little out of the money that has been spent on those two wars, other than destruction, loss of lives, the rise of terror groups, two failed states, economic chaos and misery. The conflicts have also expanded and escalated to other regions, including Syria, Libya, Somalia and Yemen—and may spread to Iran and Israel. The only accomplishment is that United States special forces have eliminated three of the world's top terrorists: Osama bin Laden, the leader of Al-Qaeda, Al-Baghdadi, the leader of ISIS, and Qasam Soleimani, the commanding general of the Iranian Revolutionary Guard's Quds Force.

The experience of violence in the 20th century is a stark reminder since it is estimated that 100 million human beings perished in wars between 1900 and 2000. Since 1945, $5 trillion has been spent on the development of nuclear weapons by the United States—an amount that could have rebuilt the entire infrastructure in the country, including homes, factories, roads, bridges, railways, airports and ship facilities. There are a number of areas in which investments can produce a great amount of innovations that can stimulate the economy in contrast to huge expenditures on wars and defense, which yield very little.

The biggest issue concerns the rising national debt. With the figure now at over $23 over trillion—an amount equal to $70,000 for every person in the United States—it is difficult to see how this will ever be significantly reduced, especially since federal spending keeps increasing. Under President Bill Clinton, the country ended with a surplus at the end of his presidency. Since that time, President George W. Bush contributed $6 trillion, President Barack Obama contributed $8 trillion, and President Donald Trump has already contributed $9 trillion. *Because of other liabilities such as Medicare and Social Security, the real level of total debt is somewhere around $75 trillion—a figure of over $225,000 per person!*

# Bibliography

"7 ways oil and gas drilling is bad for the environment". *The Wilderness Society Magazine*. August 9, 2019.

Abbott, Lewis F. *Theories of the Labour Market and Employment: A Review*. (2nd revised edition). Mountain View: Google Books, 2011.

Ampuja, Marko. *Theorizing Globalization: A Critique of the Mediatization of Social Theory*. Leiden: Brill, 2012.

Asante-Dush, K. *Public Health Risk Assessment for Human Exposure to Chemicals*. New York: Springer, 2002.

*Atkinson, A. B. (1977).* "Optimal Taxation and the Direct Versus Indirect Tax Controversy". *Canadian Journal of Economics*, 1977.

Bales, Kevin. *Modern Slavery: The Secret World of 27 Million People*. London: OneWorld Publications, 2009.

Beattie, Andrew. "How Military Spending Affects the Economy". www.investopedia.com, September 29, 2018.

Beiser, A. *Concepts of Modern Physics* (6th ed.). New York City: McGraw-Hill, 2003.

Bernstein, William. *A Splendid Exchange: How Trade Shaped the World*. New York City: Grove Press, 2008.

Borjas, George J. *Immigration Economics*. Cambridge: Harvard University Press. 2014.

Brenner, S. *Cyber Threats: The Emerging Fault Lines of the Nation State*. London: Oxford University Press, 2009.

Brezina, Corona. *Disappearing Forests: Deforestation, Desertification, and Drought*. New York: Rosen Pub Group, 2009.

Brown, Lester. *Full Planet, Empty Plates: The New Geopolitics of Food Scarcity*. New York: W. W. Norton & Company, 2012.

Brumfiel. G. "Chaos could keep fusion under control". *Nature*, May 22, 2006.

Burrows, Andrew, John Holman, Andrew Parsons, Gwen Pilling, and Gareth Price. *Chemistry.* London: Oxford University Press, 2009.

Burck, Gordon M. and Charles C. Flowerree. *International Handbook on Chemical Weapons Proliferation*. Westport: Greenwood Publishing Group, 1991.

Cantoni, L., and Danowski, J. A. (Eds.). *Communication and Technology*. Berlin: De Gruyter Mouton. 2015.

**Chaikin, Andrew**. *A Man on the Moon*. New York City: Penguin Books, 1994.

Cheney, Glenn Alan. *Lurking Doubt: Notes on Incarceration*. New London: New London Librarium, 2018.

Cirincione, Joseph. *Deadly Arsenals: Nuclear, Biological, and Chemical Threats*. Washington, D.C.: Carnegie Endowment for International Peace, 2005.

Dashevsky, Evan. "How Robots Caused Brexit and the Rise of Donald Trump" *PC Magazine*. November 8, 2017.

Easton, Mark. "What is crime?". *BBC News*. June 17, 2010.

Ehrlich, Paul R. Ehrlich & Anne H. *The Population Explosion*. London: Hutchinson, 1990.

"Emerging Pandemic Threats". www.usaid.gov. June 2, 2019.

"Environmental Impacts of Natural Gas". *Union of Concerned Scientists Magazine*. June 19, 2014.

Foskett, Janelle. "2020 Trends: Fire service leaders predict what's ahead in the new year". https://www.firerescue1.com/2019-year-review/articles/2020-trends-fire-service-leaders-predict-whats-ahead-in-the-new-year-5BUYtz3wBpfy7Od7/. December 12, 2019.

Gardner, Gerald T. *Environmental Problems and Human Behavior*. New York City: Pearson Learning Solutions, 2002.

Gierzynski, Anthony. *Saving American Elections: A Diagnosis and Prescription for a Healthier Democracy*. Amherst: Cambria Press,2011.

Gitlin, Martin. *The Arms Race and Nuclear Proliferation (Viewpoints on Modern World History)*. Farmington Hills: Greenhaven Press, 2018.

Godfrey-Smith, Peter. *Theory and Reality: An Introduction to the Philosophy of Science*, Seattle: Amazon Services LLC, 2003.

Gore, Al. *An Inconvenient Truth: The Planetary Emergency of Global Warming and What We Can Do About It*. Emmaus: Rodale Books, 2006.

Grifo, Francesca (editor) and Joshua Rosenthal (editor). *Biodiversity and Human Health*. Washington, D.C.: Island Press, 1997.

Hamblin, Jacob Darwin. *Oceanographers and the Cold War: Disciples of Marine Science*. Seattle: University of Washington Press, 2005.

Haridy, Rich. "Why do so many deadly viral outbreaks originate in bats?" www.newatlas.com. February 11, 2020.

Harwell, Mark A. *Nuclear Winter: The Human and Environmental Consequences of Nuclear War*. New York City: Springer, 1984.

Henry, P. J. and David O. Sears. *Race and Politics: The Theory of Symbolic Racism*. Berkeley: University of California Press, 2002.

Hill, Marquita K. *Understanding Environmental Pollution*. New York: Cambridge University Press, 2010.

Hosken, Fran P. "Towards a Definition of Women's Rights" in *Human Rights Quarterly*, Vol. 3, No. 2. May 1981.

Hughes, Murray. *The Second Age of Rail: A history of High-Speed Trains*. Stroud: The History Press, 2015.

Hurst, Charles E. *Social Inequality: Forms, Causes, and Consequences*. Mountain View: Google Books, 1998

"Illegal Drugs in America: A Modern History". www.Deamuseum.org

Imeson, Anton. *Desertification: Land Degradation and Sustainability*. New York: Wiley, 2011.

International Renewable Energy Agency. *Global Energy Transformation: A Roadmap to 2050*. Abu Dhabi: IRENA, 2019.

Jacobson, Mark Z. "The 7 reasons why nuclear energy is not the answer to solve climate change". www.leonardodecaprio.org. June 20, 2019.

Jordan, David, James D. Kiras, David J. Lonsdale, Ian Speller, Christopher Tuck and C. Dale Walton. *Understanding Modern Warfare*. New York: Cambridge University Press, 2008.

Kaltenegger, Lisa, et al. "Greenhouse Effect", *Encyclopedia of Astrobiology*.

Kelley T. "Bats Perish, and No One Knows Why". *The New York Times*, March 25, 2008.

Kisak, Paul F., editor. *Nuclear Terrorism & the Dirty Bomb: "A Clear and Present Danger"(The Nuclear Threat) (Volume 4)*. Seattle: Createspace, 2017

Koh, Jae Myong/ *Green Infrastructure Financing: Institutional Investors, PPPs and Bankable Projects*, London: Palgrave Macmillan, 2018.

Krishnamurti, Jiddu. *On Education*. New York City: Harper & Row Publishers, 1974.

Ksir, Oakley and Charles Ray. *Drugs, society, and human behavior*(9th ed.). New York City: McGraw-Hill, 2002.

Kunich, John Charles. Killing Our Oceans: Dealing with the Mass Extinction of Marine Life. Santa Barbara: Praeger, 2006.

Laplante, Phillip. *What Every Engineer Should Know about Software Engineering*. Boca Raton: CRC, 2007.

Larson, Edward J. *Evolution: The Remarkable History of a Scientific Theory*. New York City: Random House Publishing Group, 2006.

Leonard K. "Could Universal Health Care Save U.S. Taxpayers Money?". *U.S. News & World Report*. January 22, 2016

Linkletter, David. "The 10 Biggest Math Breakthroughs of 2019". *Popular Mechanics,* December 27, 2019.

Litt, Robert S. "Privacy, Technology and National Security". www.intelligence.gov.

Maennling, Nicolas and Perrine Toledano. "Seven trends shaping the future of the mining and metals industry". https://www.weforum.org/agenda/2019/03/seven-trends-shaping-the-future-of-the-mining-and-metals-sector/, March 29, 2019.

Mahar, Maggie, *Money-Driven Medicine: The Real Reason Health Care Costs So Much*. New York City: Harper/Collins, 2006.

Maslin, Mark. *Climate Change: A Very Short Introduction*. London: Oxford University Press, 2014.

McCallum, M. L. "Amphibian Decline or Extinction? Current Declines Dwarf Background Extinction Rate". *Journal of Herpetology,* 2007.

McCorduck, Pamela. *Machines Who Think* (2nd ed.). Natick: A. K. Peters, Ltd., 2004.

Meigs, James B. "The Myth of Clean Coal: Analysis". *Popular Mechanics Magazine*. July 14, 2011.

"Mental Illness: Special Form of RNA in the Brain". University of New Mexico Health Sciences Center. www.sciencedaily.com. February 12, 2020.

Moskowitz, Sanford L. *Advanced Materials Innovation: Managing Global Technology in the 21st century*. New York City: John Wiley & Sons, 2016.

Newman, D. M. *Sociology : exploring the architecture of everyday life* (9th ed.). Los Angeles: SAGE, 2012.

Nierenberg, Danielle. *State of the World 2006: a Worldwatch Institute report on progress toward a sustainable society*. New York: W.W. Norton, 2006.

Nocks, Lisa. *The Robot : The Life Story of a Technology.* Westport: Greenwood Publishing Group, 2007.

Nordrum, Amy and Clark, Kristen. "Everything you need to know about 5G". *IEEE Spectrum Magazine*. January 27, 2017.

Oldroyd, Benjamin P. "What's Killing American Honey Bees?". *PLoS Biology*, 2007.

"Opioids". *Drugs of Abuse*. National Institute on Drug Abuse. 2019.

Pradesh, Uttar. "Poverty, Growth and Inequality". World Bank Group. www.worldbank.org. July 5, 2019.

Prud'homme, Alex. *The Ripple Effect: The Fate of Freshwater in the Twenty-First Century*. New York City: Scribner, 2012.

Rockwell, Garrett. *A Food Shortage Is Coming: The Imminent And Impending Doom Of Our Civilization*. Malden: PublishMyWay, 2014.

Roulstone, Ian and John Norbury. *Invisible in the Storm: The Role of Mathematics in Understanding Weather*. Princeton: Princeton University Press, 2013.

Ruddiman, William F. *Earth's Climate: Past and Future*. New York City: W. H. Freeman and Company, 2008.

Sagan, Scott Douglas and Kenneth N. Waltz. *The Spread of Nuclear Weapons: An Enduring Debate*. New York City: W. W. Norton & Company, 2012.

Simon, Seymour. *Global Warming*. New York City: HarperCollins, 2013.

Smith, Jeffrey M. *Seeds of Destruction: Exposing Industry and Government Lies About the Safety of the Genetically Engineered Foods You're Eating*. Portland: Yes! Books, 2003.

Squires, Peter. *Gun Crime in Global Contexts*. London: Routledge, 2014.

"The Role and Responsibilities of the Police". Policy Studies Institute. December 12, 2009.

Vandenbosch, Robert and Susanne E. Vandenbosch. *Nuclear Waste Stalemate*. Salt Lake City: University of Utah Press, 2007.

Van Wyck, Peter C. *Signs Of Danger: Waste, Trauma, and Nuclear Threat*. Minneapolis: University Of Minnesota Press, 2004.

Weil, David N. "The Economics of Population Aging" in Mark R. Rosenzweig and Oded Stark, editors. *Handbook of Population and Family Economics*. New York City: Elsevier, 1997.

West, Darrell. *"Will robots and AI take your job? The economic and political consequences of automation"* Brookings Institute. April 18, 2018.

Wheelis M, Rozsa L, Dando M (2006). *Deadly Cultures: Biological Weapons Since 1945*. Harvard University Press.

White, Debra. "Pros and Cons of Legalizing Marijuana in the U.S.". www.thoughtco.com. February 5, 2020.

Young. E.M. *Food and Development*. Abingdon: Routledge, 2012.

Zarocostas, John. "Proliferation of firearms is a growing global health problem". www.ncbi.nih.gov. September 8, 2007.

www.ingramcontent.com/pod-product-compliance
Lightning Source LLC
Chambersburg PA
CBHW081429220526
45466CB00008B/2324